UNWHITE ▶

THE SOUTH ON SCREEN

EDITED BY R. Barton Palmer and Matthew H. Bernstein

UNWHITE

Appalachia, Race, and Film ► Meredith McCarroll

THE UNIVERSITY OF GEORGIA PRESS   ATHENS

© 2018 by the University of Georgia Press
Athens, Georgia 30602
www.ugapress.org
All rights reserved
Set in 10/14 Warnock and Helvetica Neue by
Graphic Composition, Inc., Bogart, GA.

Most University of Georgia Press titles are
available from popular e-book vendors.

Printed digitally

Library of Congress Cataloging-in-Publication Data

NAMES: McCarroll, Meredith, author.
TITLE: Unwhite : Appalachia, race, and film / Meredith McCarroll.
DESCRIPTION: Athens : The University of Georgia Press, [2018] |
     Series: South on screen series
IDENTIFIERS: LCCN 2018003948| ISBN 9780820353364 (hardcover : alk. paper) |
     ISBN 9780820353623 (pbk. : alk. paper) | ISBN 9780820353371 (ebook)
SUBJECTS: LCSH: Appalachians (People) in motion pictures. | Whites in motion pictures. |
     Race relations in motion pictures. | Other (Philosophy) in motion pictures. |
     Southern States—In motion pictures.
CLASSIFICATION: LCC PN1995.9.M67 M33 2018 | DDC 791.4308991607—dc23
LC record available at https://lccn.loc.gov/2018003948

For my mama.

Contents

Acknowledgments

hip Arnold and Lynn Sanders first helped me see myself as Appalachian, and each gave me the tools and language to think critically about what that might mean. To you both I am grateful.

Thanks go to Barton Palmer, who said I could write a book and told me to go do it. Colleagues at two institutions talked to me over many beers, asked how the writing was going, and created space for me to work on this project. Special thanks go to Jonathan Beecher Field, Sarah Juliet Lauro, Michael LeMahieu, Amy Monaghan, and Brandon Turner for that work. To the many people who read or heard versions of this book in process, I am grateful: Mary Anglin, Sandy Ballard, Keely Byars-Nichols, Anna Creadick, Parker Essick, Phil Obermiller, Doug Reichert Powell, Emily Satterwhite, Barbara Ellen Smith, and Jerry Williamson. Thanks also go to my colleagues at Bowdoin College, who asked the right questions and made the right pushes, especially Brock Clarke, who knew when to tell me to stop writing.

Research for this book was made possible through grants and funding from the Clemson University Humanities Advancement Board Collaborative Research Grant, Clemson University Digital Humanities Initiative Seed Grant Program, Clemson University Pearce Center Research Grant, Bowdoin College, and the Appalachian Studies

Association. Many thanks to ASA for providing a space for scholars to realize that this is a field, for maintaining high expectations of its members, and for reminding us all why Appalachia is worth thinking about. Thanks go, especially, to ASA and the Wilma Dykeman Faces of Appalachia Postdoctoral Research Fellowship for financial support during this process. Walter Biggins was an amazing teacher and editor, walking me through this new process with patience and enthusiasm. Thanks too to Ana Jimenez-Moreno, Susan Silver, and Thomas Roche, for all that they did behind the scenes to turn this into an actual book.

I especially thank my mother, Phyllis Braswell, for first encouraging me to ask questions and my brother, Matt McCarroll, for showing me to always doubt easy answers. To the friends and family who kept asking how the book was coming, thank you. For those who offered quiet spaces to write and free child care, this book wouldn't exist without you.

For their immeasurable understanding, independence, interest, and good humor, this book is for Jeff, Jasper, and Townes. These ideas and this manuscript moved with us to four addresses and required more nurturing than I'm proud to admit. Simply put, thank you for loving me through it.

UNWHITE ▶

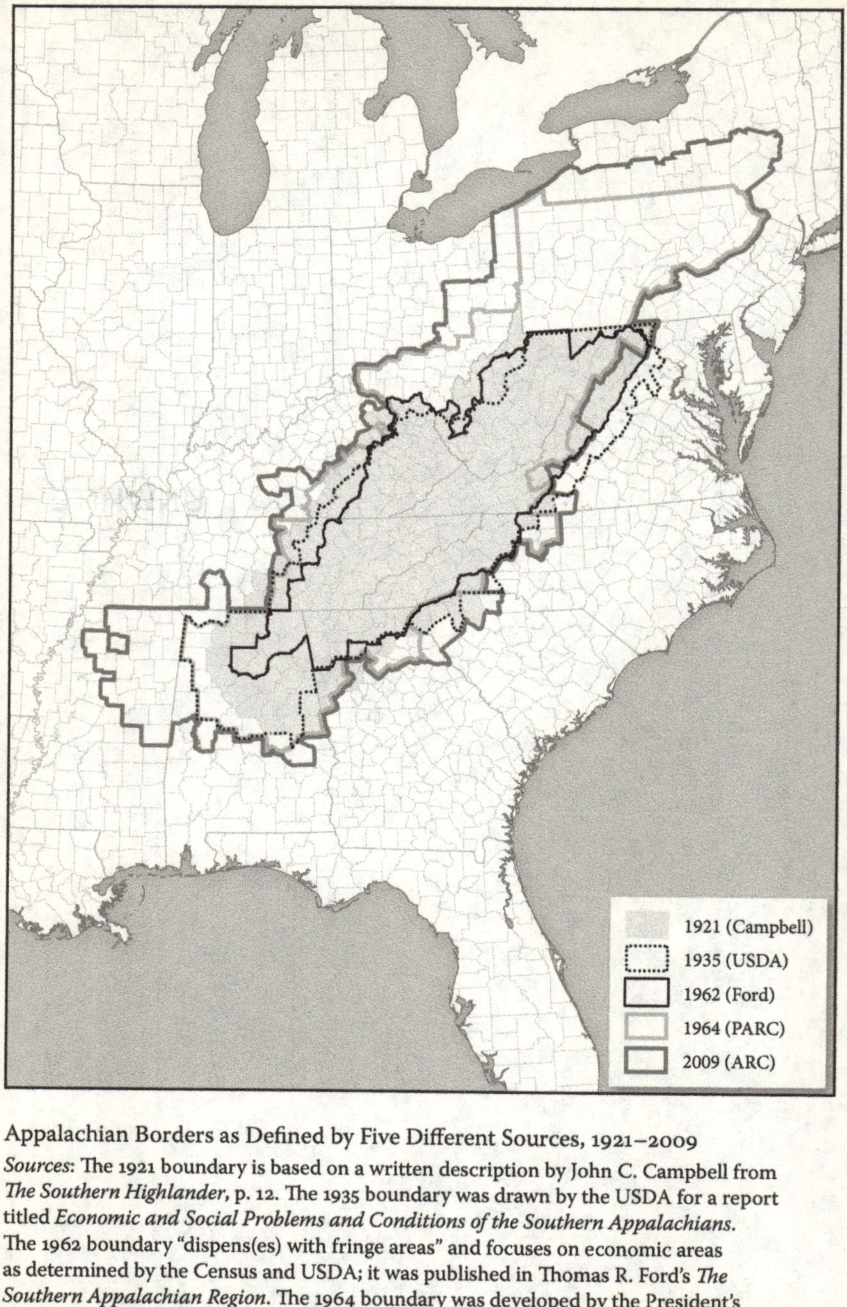

1921 (Campbell)
1935 (USDA)
1962 (Ford)
1964 (PARC)
2009 (ARC)

Appalachian Borders as Defined by Five Different Sources, 1921–2009

Sources: The 1921 boundary is based on a written description by John C. Campbell from *The Southern Highlander*, p. 12. The 1935 boundary was drawn by the USDA for a report titled *Economic and Social Problems and Conditions of the Southern Appalachians*. The 1962 boundary "dispens(es) with fringe areas" and focuses on economic areas as determined by the Census and USDA; it was published in Thomas R. Ford's *The Southern Appalachian Region*. The 1964 boundary was developed by the President's Appalachian Regional Commission and is available at arc.gov. The 2009 boundary is included in the most recent remapping by the Appalachian Regional Commission based on economic and transportation data and is also available at arc.gov.

Introduction

I did not become Appalachian until I left home. Or, rather, I did not understand myself to be Appalachian until I left home. I first caught a glimpse in college, as I positively identified with the region during a course called Experiencing Appalachia. I was still in Appalachia, attending Appalachian State University, and the term *Appalachian*—though relatively new to me—was broad, multifaceted, and evolving. It was when I left the region that I began to understand how my Appalachian identity marked me in the broader culture, and it seemed that this marking was shaped predominantly by movies.

I had come to use the term *Appalachian* rather than, or in addition to, *southern* because it was a better fit. Mountain culture shaped my values and my accent, and I liked the shape that it had taken. I was surprised when, living in different parts of the country, I was forced to see myself as others seemed to see me. I was forced to see Appalachia as others did. As I introduced myself in my new homes—first in Los Angeles and then in Boston—I was frequently answered with the banjo licks from *Deliverance*. These interactions were puzzling to me, as someone who had seen *Deliverance*, had grown up near the river where it was filmed, and understood it to be a horror film rather than a documentary. Had they seen the movie? Were they really trying to equate me somehow with that banjo-playing kid because I was from Appalachia? It was a strange interaction, repeated enough to give me pause. It happens still, in my most recent home in Maine. The word *Appalachia* triggers a Pavlovian banjo impersonation tied to images of depravity and violence.

Over the years I have navigated different positions to either combat these generalizations or distance myself from them. What has been consistent, though, is the reliance on film to respond to the region. It was in reaction to these responses that I began to write this book. Initially, I wanted to show how diverse the region was by culling the various portrayals of Appalachia to complicate and diffuse the power of *Deliverance*. The more I watched, though, the more patterns of representation emerged. What I'd hoped would be a complex web of images instead grouped together in ways I couldn't unsee. Appalachians were being portrayed using the same lazy methods that had long since been used to portray nonwhites, effectively disempowering through generalized degrading images. As patterns emerged, motivations and stakes came into question, and the project became much trickier than I had imagined it to be.

Even—and perhaps most especially—from the vantage point of the already *othered* southerner, Appalachian identity can be seen as a unique form of otherness. My work aims to understand the function of the *other* through a historicized racial lens, specifically interrogating the investment in Appalachia as poor and white. Drawing from critical race theory and film studies, I assert that Appalachia is represented by familiar tropes long used to present the nonwhite and to make evident the split between self and other, hero and outlier. At once the images are phenotypically white and hierarchically nonwhite. The term *unwhite* draws attention to the simultaneous assumption of and exclusion from an imagined community of whiteness and to the investment in the protection of whiteness.

Appalachia resides in the American imagination at the intersections of race and class. There is a deep historical investment in seeing the region as "pure white stock" *and* as deeply impoverished and backward. The popularity of J. D. Vance's *Hillbilly Elegy* (2016) speaks to an interest in the ways that racial privilege and economic disadvantage collide in this region, but it speaks especially to a desire for an easy explanation. A memoir emphasizing the rise of author J. D. Vance from impoverished Ohio to Yale Law School, drawing heavily on his family ties to Kentucky, *Hillbilly Elegy* provides an answer, blaming the victims for allowing their poverty to happen to them. In 1965 *The Negro*

Family: The Case for National Action, written by then–assistant secretary of labor Daniel Patrick Moynihan and commonly known as the Moynihan Report, asserted the negative correlation between welfare and intact black families and, in assigning responsibility for poverty to black family structures, effectively blamed the victims for their condition. Similarly, in *Hillbilly Elegy*, Vance concludes that it is the hillbilly who is to blame for his continued depravity. Vance assures his readers that "there is no government that can fix these problems for us. . . . We created them, and only we can fix them" (256).

Following the publication of the Moynihan Report, William Ryan wrote *Blaming the Victim* (1976) as a critique of the report, calling out the conclusions as an intentional affront to the civil rights movement. Ryan took issue with the way that the readers of the Moynihan Report diverted responsibility from systems of oppression and placed it squarely on the oppressed. This is precisely the appeal of *Hillbilly Elegy*, offering an explanation with no expectation. The reception of *Hillbilly Elegy* has, of course, not been purely positive. Many have challenged both Vance's claims and the reliance on these claims as an explanation for everything from the rise in opioid use in Appalachia to the election of Donald Trump as president of the United States (MacGillis 2016; S. Jones 2016).

In a review that refers to *Hillbilly Elegy* as the "pejorative Moynihan report on the black family in white face," Dwight Billings (2016) points to the shortcomings of the book in a way that ties the book's reception to my project—helping me understand my own irrational and emotional dislike for the book. Billings writes, "It is one thing to write a personal memoir but quite something else—something exceedingly audacious—to presume to write the 'memoir' of a culture." To write the memoir of a culture is certainly audacious. To buy and believe in a memoir of a culture reveals acutely the readiness to essentialize a region and to blame the victim. I don't disagree with Vance that there is work that "we" can do to fix the problems of the region. I take seriously, though, Vance's ignorant avoidance of organizations, activists, writers, and artists from Appalachia who are doing all kinds of things to fix its problems. And I take seriously the failure of federal organizations to attend to Appalachia.

Perhaps I should take on *Hillbilly Elegy*, as it sits atop best-seller lists and replaces *Deliverance* in conversations with folks who hear I'm from Appalachia. Far more than *Deliverance*, *Hillbilly Elegy* is granting talking points and assuredness to readers who sometimes lecture me now about the problems of my region, holding tight to J. D. Vance's hand as he serves as an eager tour guide relying only on his individual experience. Instead, though, I choose to see the connection between these moments of reception and am eager to hold viewers and readers accountable for their participation in the cycle of creation and consumption that solidifies perceptions into realities. This study not only calls out writers like J. D. Vance, who present a metonymic explanation of a complex region, but also pushes readers and viewers to examine the appeal of these images. This book asks its readers to question what is at stake in simplistic and demeaning representations of a diverse population and region. It asks readers to understand the ways that *Deliverance* and *Hillbilly Elegy* serve a similar purpose—*othering* Appalachia in both romanticizing and demonizing ways, especially when read as representative of a region. To keep believing stories like these, which give the government permission to look away and step back, a powerful cultural image is constructed, distributed, and consumed across popular culture.

A complex debate—at least within Appalachian studies—surrounds the role of hillbillies as objects of ridicule and critique. As Matthew Ferrence argues in *All-American Redneck: Variations on an Icon, from James Fenimore Cooper to the Dixie Chicks*, "Despite the lack of precision in the word *redneck*, few people would pause for more than a breath when asked to describe one. They know, we all know, what a redneck *is*, because we've all seen them before within the collective cultural history of the nation" (2014, 16). I would argue that we not only know what a redneck is; we depend on the existence of the redneck. Further, we recognize and depend on the existence of Appalachia, which has also been represented in the "collective cultural history." There is a need, it seems, to distinguish the lowest, the poorest, the most ignorant . . . the most laughable. There is a need for an *other*.[1] In *Southern Folk, Plain and Fancy*, John Shelton Reed notes that in media images and popular culture "hillbillies appear to be the last acceptable ethnic fools" (1986, 43). Appalachia, following Reed's (contested) logic, may be the last safe space to mock.

Barbara Ellen Smith boldly challenges this notion, driven by the risk that to make that claim is to take the "inaccurate and highly misleading position that 'hillbillies' are, in effect, a racial minority" (2004, 39). Informed by this debate over Appalachian identity politics and the risks of eliding generalized regional representation with racial oppression, I enter this conversation intending to answer John Hartigan's call for a "mode of analysis that distinguishes between racial dynamics and the national and local or regional levels" while remaining "attentive both to broader dynamics of racial formation and to the varieties or twists that remake or transform those dynamics in particular locales" (2004, 70; see also "Appalachian Identity" 2010). I am interested in the stakes of cinematic images of Appalachian figures that are almost exclusively phenotypically white, while relying on tropes long used to depict nonwhites. Appalachia, therefore, exists in the imagination of many passive consumers of these depictions as somewhere between white and nonwhite. The term *unwhite*, I hope, evokes this precariously constructed position that at once relies on *othering* and erases its racial context.

The tension between a Hollywood that insists on the whiteness of Appalachia but relies on nonwhite figurings of Appalachians provokes the assumption that white privilege is somehow kept out of the region. My argument depends on the dual notion that Appalachia has been racialized and *othered* in film *and* that white privilege pervades even in situations of white poverty. It is the tension between a diverse and broadly defined region and its simplistic portrayal that compels this study; it is the complex reality of white privilege and demeaning regional stereotyping that offer points of entry. This book acknowledges and engages with the ways that Appalachia might, in fact, be a remaining "safe" stereotype while actively resisting the notion that this makes Appalachians similar to those who have been systemically and legally oppressed because of race.

At the point of convergence between critical race studies and cinema studies, important work by scholars in the 1980s and 1990s made evident the detrimental impact of narrow typing and reliance on caricature in the portrayal of African Americans and Native Americans.[2] The linkage between representation, perception, and identity became a crucial conversation in these fields. What we see in film shapes what we understand of those onscreen. As Karen L. Cox asserts in *Dreaming of Dixie*, "Movies revolutionized how different communities of Americans perceived one another and influenced their opinions on race, class, ethnicity, and even different regions of the country" (2011, 82). The more visible the difference, the more easily the caricature is built. Scholars like Donald Bogle, bell hooks, Michael Hilger, and Philip Deloria have revealed the uses and abuses of portrayals of Mexican Americans, Asian Americans, Indian Americans, Arab Americans, and other minority groups who have been considered racial others (Rodriquez 2004; Ono and Pham 2009; Shaheen 2009; Hilger 1995). Turning the critical race lens toward white objects, scholars and viewers look closely at the construction of whiteness in film and literature, based on the idea that to notice only the construction of nonwhites is to privilege and normalize white representations—as if they were not constructed. Critical whiteness studies scholars such as David Roediger and George Lipsitz look closely at the intersection of race and class, lending perspective to the emerging field of critical study about "white trash" culture and "Grit Lit," which has placed the proud redneck claims of Larry the Cable Guy, Lewis Grizzard, and Jeff Foxworthy under the microscope to understand the intersection between white privilege, poverty, and regional identity (Wray 2006).[3] Borrowing more from Marxist than Girls Raised in the South (GRITS) ideology, critical work on race, place, and class has begun to develop in relation to earlier questions about representations of the *other* situated on nonwhite bodies and experiences.[4]

In the preface of his important study *All That Is Native and Fine*, David Whisnant explains his intentions as he writes about the role of "culture workers" who traveled to and helped shape Appalachia. The impact of these visitors, who founded settlement schools and folk festivals and art schools, was physical, ideological, and representational—whether that was the intention or not. Reflecting on this, Whisnant writes, "This is a book about cultural 'otherness,' about how people perceive each other across cultural boundaries—especially those boundaries that correlate with social class. It is also about cultural anxiety, cultural manipulation, cultural change, and cultural survival (and *re*-vival). It is about cultural assumptions and cultural images, about the purposeful translation and willful transformation of culture" (1983, xxxv). As I write about films portraying the Appalachian Mountains, I too intend to point to the manipulation of images while resisting the temptation to victimize the people of the region. This complex relationship between representation and identity presents challenges but will ground the value and integrity of a complicated answer over the simplicity of a myopic perspective.

This book is about the precarious position of Appalachia in Hollywood cinema, which both reifies a racist hierarchy through its reliance on familiar tropes of representation and conveys a false notion of a racially monolithic region. This book confirms that white privilege makes its way across class lines in a culture where race trumps class. And it is a book that asks what is at stake in the continued representations of a global Appalachia that relies on racialized stereotypes from the turn of the past century.

▶ Appalachia

When I first conceived of the idea for this book project, I visited the W. L. Eury Appalachian Collection at Appalachian State University and met with librarian Fred Hay, who asked me an important question that I could not answer: "Which definition of Appalachia are you using?" When it was evident that I did not understand his question, he showed me the *Appalachian Region Borders*, a composite map that clearly demonstrates the various definitions of Appalachia by overlaying five maps of Appalachian borders drawn at dates ranging from 1921 to 1967 by mapmakers employed by the USDA, the Appalachian Regional Commission, and others.[5] (See the map facing page 1 for a revised version of this composite rendering of the region's borders.) To define a place is both to consider geography and to think about culture. In the case of Appalachia, neither a clear map nor a list of cultural characteristics is evident. While the same may be said of many regions, the difficulty to define Appalachia has itself become a defining characteristic.[6]

The defining of Appalachia began before the earliest dates on the compilation map, and points to the consistent inability to say what is or isn't Appalachia. In 1895 Berea College president William G. Frost worked to formally define "Appalachian America" using geologic characteristics (cited in J. Williams 2001, 12).[7] In 1921 John Charles Campbell, in *The Southern Highlander and His Homeland*, used the Mason-Dixon Line, the Ohio River, and the Blue Ridge Mountains to delineate the region, relying on behavior as much as landscape.[8] By the 1960s, with the creation of the Appalachian Regional Commission, the definition of Appalachia had become politicized, linked closely to resources and need.[9] Inclusion by the commission gave counties access to grants but left them vulnerable to judgment. A decade later, in "Toward a Natural Delineation of the Area Known as the Southern Appalachian Highlands," D. S. Blauch overviews the range of definitions of Appalachia, calling for a new definition in 1975 based on botanical, rather than geologic, properties.[10]

Zoom in to any of these moments, and contradictory and simultaneous definitions of the region emerge. In the 1930s, for example, the Southern Highlands Craft Guild loosely defined the region to be inclusive of artists in boundary counties, fully embracing that cultural impact that does not cease at county lines. Meanwhile, the Bureau of Agricultural Economics divided Appalachia into two subregions to best support and advise those working within the agricultural industry. Tiered definitions like this served a different purpose for the bureau than for the craft guild. The bureau needed to emphasize the differences in terrain, whereas the guild needed to see the broad diaspora of folkways. This example and others serve to demonstrate the various ways that the region has been defined; where and what counts as Appalachian is up to the definer. These maps, these definitions, and these arguments over who counts and what it all means leads someone like Douglas Reichert Powell to resist new maps, to mute unresolved border disputes, and to trust instincts. If looking for Appalachia, "we see it when we know it," he told me on May 22, 2017. What we see and what we know, though, are often decided by filmmakers, photographers, and journalists who have less at stake when they show us Appalachia.

If I must answer the question about which Appalachia I mean, I turn to John Alexander Williams, whose "Appalachian History: Regional History in the Post-Modern Zone" offers a guide through these controversies over defining Appalachia, finally asserting the following definition of Appalachia: "What all definitions of Appalachia have in common is that each of them in its way tries to link people and homeland, to find some principle of regional demarcation that identifies both the place and its people. My approach is no different, except in one important respect. I prefer a dynamic definition of Appalachia and its people as both have changed through time" (2001, 181). I seek an Appalachia with a dynamic definition still finite enough to be a definition. For this book this means that I have relaxed my geographic boundaries and tried to pay attention to perceptive boundaries. So many people asked me about Debra Granik's 2010 film *Winter's Bone* that I stopped explaining the Ozarks and started seeing it as an Appalachian film.[11] If a film was marketed as a "Southern Mountain" film, is clearly set in Appalachia, is based on a book in Appalachia, or is overwhelmingly perceived as Appalachian, I'm counting it as Appalachian. After months of thinking through how to define the region for this book, I realized that the reason I was writing the book all along is that others are already defining it. For once I'll let them.

▶ Race

African Americans are no more monolithic than Anglo Americans; Hispanic Americans are as diverse as "whites." Notably, though, there are no books on white types in film, while there are widely shared ideas about the few stereotypes used to represent nonwhite groups in Hollywood. There is now, in your hands, a book about the stereotypes used to represent Appalachia in Hollywood (contributing to an already-established conversation[12]) because, as the mainstream culture industry has shown with African Americans, Hispanic Americans, and Native Americans, it believes that it knows well enough how to portray these types. To do so is to rely on types that work to disempower, simplify, and continue to other. It is a lazy form of representation, but it is more than that. It is a damning generalization that enables conversations like the ones I keep having about *Deliverance* and *Hillbilly Elegy* and that enlivens assumptions about groups bound by geography.

As whiteness studies developed, the goals of particular schools and scholars diverged.[13] The constructedness of whiteness, the mythology of whiteness, and the perpetuation of whiteness all depend on the invisibility of whiteness. A cycle of creation and consumption maintains white privilege and sustains a racialized hierarchy. Beyond an acknowledgment that race is constructed and that mythologized whiteness is silently perpetuated as normal, there is a complex system that marks Appalachia as *other*, while consistently portraying Appalachians as white. Just as (often as) unconscious efforts normalize whiteness, similar efforts situate Appalachia as outside, stabilizing the non-Appalachian as natural and correct. The construction, mythology, and perpetuation of nonwhiteness maintains racial hierarchies, and the construction, mythology, and perpetuation of Appalachia as outside of the mainstream strengthens a regional hierarchy, using the racialized representations in covert and powerful ways.

An emerging critical school in the 1990s began to evaluate literary and cinematic representations of whiteness. In *Playing in the Dark: Whiteness and the Literary Imagination*, Toni Morrison calls for readers and scholars to acknowledge the pervasiveness of literary whiteness to see the ways that it has become "'universal' or race-free" (1992, xii). Building on the well-established perspective that race is constructed in its own particular geographic and political moment, sociologists and race scholars Michael Omi and Howard Winant analyze the processes through which the meanings of race are established, which they call "racialization." Racialization emphasizes characteristics that mark races as unique. An extension of their thinking allows us to understand a process of regionalization—establishing the meanings of different regions. Like racialization, there is value in understanding the unique characteristics that differentiate one from another. In Omi and Winant, however, there is an awareness that whiteness is exempted from the process of racialization (2014, 49). The normalcy of whiteness depends on the existence of racialized others. Similarly, the America exempted from regionalization depends on *othered* regions to lend stability to the norm.

In his 1997 book, *White*, Richard Dyer explains, "White power none the less reproduces itself regardless of the intention, power differences, and goodwill, and overwhelmingly because it is not seen as whiteness, but as normal.

White people need to learn to see themselves as white, to see their particularity. In other words, whiteness needs to be made strange" (10). If whiteness needs to be made strange, then what are we to do with the already bizarrely depicted Appalachia? Following Dyer's call, we need to see Appalachia rather than assume that we already understand it. Even if the assumption is that Appalachia is strange, that strangeness requires interrogation.

The ways that whiteness "reproduces itself" are necessarily subtle, relying on invisibility for the perception of normativity. As Dyer points out, the reproduction of the myth of white normativity is generally unconscious. Whether conscious or not, one of the primary reasons that whiteness maintains its dominant position is due to what George Lipsitz calls the "possessive investment in whiteness." Lipsitz calls for whites to acknowledge that they are a part of the problem "not because of our race, but because of our possessive investment in it" (1995, 384). The investment in whiteness is due to ways that whites, overtly or covertly, have been encouraged to invest in the belief that whiteness is superior and that whites are somehow deserving of their elevated social status. White people, through careful narratives and the perpetuation of myths, claim "family values, fatherhood and foresight" rather than "favoritism," creating the sense that whites have earned their privileges (380). There is a logical extension to regionalism—and an investment in the "standard" values, accents, landscapes—stripped of history and accuracy. America is seen as multicultural, made of distinct regions and people with various races. Simultaneously, though, the favored race and the favored region can exist only in contrast to other less favored races and regions.

In "Whiteness and Appalachian Studies: What's the Connection?" John Hartigan Jr. admits a "somewhat critical stance towards the field of whiteness studies" and asserts that the claims that mountain whites are racially subordinate carries a "huge emotional and intellectual charge that makes their conclusions and implications difficult for some to accept; as well, the subject in question, whiteness, is notoriously elusive and difficult to grasp" (2004, 58). It is precisely this elusive nature that gives power to the position of whiteness. Clarity of definition relies on simplified perception. The more difficult a group is to define, the more resistant it is to stereotyping.

White privilege is granted based on phenotype and transcends class distinctions. According to Peggy McIntosh (2001), race is a powerful marker, one more permanent and visible than socioeconomic status. In her piece "Explaining White Privilege to a Broke White Person," Gina Crosley-Corcoran (2014) discusses her experiences as a white impoverished young person. She relies on the concept of intersectionality to understand the ways that she *is* and *is not* privileged. Crosley-Corcoran initially criticized McIntosh for conflating class with race: "When I first wrote about White Privilege years ago, I demanded to know why this White Woman felt that my experiences were the same as hers when no, my family most certainly could not rent housing *'in an area which we could afford and want to live.'*" She acknowledges, though, that she does have access to privileges based on her race, if not her class. These are the "unearned benefits" that McIntosh outlines, and that do make their way into Appalachia . . . but not fully. As Crosley-Corcoran points out, there are other factors that limit one's privilege. One of them is region. An individual from Appalachia may have class, gender, and race privilege, but according to the power of stereotypes, they are seen and represented as *other*, with less privilege. Theories of white privilege assert that my white neighbor in western North Carolina can walk into a store without suspicion of shoplifting. A number of factors—including class—might determine that this white neighbor would be viewed with suspicion. Her race, though, would not be one of the factors. Her whiteness would privilege her.

As I look at race in Appalachia from the perspective of perception rather than reality, I navigate contentious waters. Scholars such as William Turner and Edward J. Cabbell (1985) and John Inscoe (2005) have written about the racial diversity of the region, and their results work to break up the misconception of Appalachia as a racial monolith. Although there is growing ethnic and racial diversity in Appalachia, the image of Appalachia is consistently white, poor, and undereducated. I depend on these misrepresentations to support the idea that region and race intersect to shape the perceptions and, by extension, the lived experiences of mountaineers.

Jerry Williamson's extensive *Southern Mountaineers Filmography* (1995b), a catalog of more than a thousand films released between 1903 and 1994, is a productive site to mine for the differences in representation and the reality of the census.[14] My work to extend Williamson's catalog to the present demonstrates that fewer than thirty of the films include any Appalachian figures of color. The continued portrayal of the region as monolithic in terms of race, class, and education level demonstrates the investment in a generalized image of Appalachia that can be dismissed as outside of the norm. Complications of the region from any of these points of entry make such a quick dismissal difficult.

Scholars such as Darlene Wilson, Matt Wray, John Hartigan, and Barbara Ellen Smith have explored whiteness in Appalachia with attention to constructions of whiteness.[15] In her analysis of John Fox Jr., Wilson argues that the purpose of his work "has been to racialize the 'southern mountaineer' within an evolving national text as 'almost-white,' a regional 'other' historically bound to pathological, under-class status." Wilson's work on Fox is an important influence, as I broaden her reading across the history of Hollywood cinematic representation. Wilson makes clear in her work that the consistent images of Appalachia as outside the norm mark a "felicitous convergence of mythmaking and capital accumulation" (1995, 8). For Wilson, Fox's work consistently keeps the Appalachian figure just outside of the norm. "He helped to create and/or perpetuate myths of Appalachian 'otherness' for two purposes that can be traced within his texts and journals: 1) to facilitate corporate and class hegemony by marginalizing indigenous peoples and existing socio-cultural structures, and 2) to undermine local resistance to the 'new order' and to absentee control by implementing land and political policies that encouraged depopulation" (7). In many ways, I agree with Wilson about how representation functions to *other* in these specific systemic ways. The term *unwhite* resonates with me and feels like an important addition to the conversation because the patterns of representation are so closely tied to representation of nonwhites. When looking broadly at Appalachia on film, it is not merely that Appalachia is outside of the norm but rather that the very same generalizations that have been used in film to disempower nonwhites are actively used in the representation of Appalachians.

There remains space to offer a reading of whiteness as it intersects with regional identity; the presence of scholarship conveys the unresolved ideas around the topic. Too often Appalachian scholars have left race entirely out of conversations of the region, relying themselves on white privilege. When undefined, the subjects are assumed to be white. I am inspired by Barbara Ellen Smith's (2004) call to avoid falling into the trap of seeing Appalachians as a minority in a way that is grounded in white privilege itself. Situating cinematic representations of Appalachia within critical race theory and whiteness studies allows deeper issues of power to come into focus.

The language of critical race studies builds the vocabulary with which we can speak about power and representation in Appalachia. I frame this argument about Appalachian representations through critical race theory and whiteness studies because of the ways that it grounds the representations within an established field of study, built on questions of power and difference. The images of Appalachia as *other* are deeply rooted in a maintenance of white normative privilege. There exist films set in Appalachia that offer a range of complex figures from the region or tend to explore the various strata of its populace. In his review of the 2015 film *Big Stone Gap*, author Silas House points out how remarkable it is to find films that resist the traditional negative depictions, claiming that this film "did something no movie ever has: showed Appalachia as a place of both diversity and intelligence." These were not the films that come to the minds of my Boston colleagues when I said that I am from the North Carolina mountains, though. The complex images and depictions are sparse compared to the plentiful stereotyped images that spring to the minds of most Americans when Appalachia is mentioned. It is these images, always phenotypically white, with which I am concerned and on which I will focus. It is these images that align closely with the representations of nonwhites, which have, for a century, been used to demean, alienate, make comic, demonize, and otherwise place the nonwhite subject in an alterior position. This nonwhite typing conflates with portrayals of consistently white individuals, placing them in the position of the *unwhite*. Seeking to explore the presence and the limits of white privilege in Appalachian film, I intend the term *unwhite* to disrupt assumptions, evoking both the self and the other position in its very name. To name the Appalachian figure as *unwhite* is to show, I hope, the duality of the position, the lasting privilege of whiteness, and the necessity to mark as *unwhite* that figure that does not belong.

Film

The borders of Appalachia have been contested, shifted, redrawn, and made permeable in much the same way as the borders of racial categories. Neither can be proven, and both are relative. Both have been actively constructed, with similar stakes. James Baldwin and Ronald Eller each claim the need for a racial other to define a self.[16] We know who we are only when we know who we are not. I traverse this space carefully, with an awareness of its risks. My argument about race and the representation of Appalachia is at once very simple and complicated enough to warrant careful explanation. In short, Appalachia has been portrayed as monolithically white, despite the actual racial and ethnic diversity of the region. At the same time, though, most depictions of Appalachia rely on narrow and derogatory stereotypes based on the tropes long used to depict nonwhites in film. With pressure from both sides, the result is a set of representations that I call *unwhite*: images that are phenotypically white and drawn from nonwhite stereotypes, which seem to categorize Appalachia outside of white normative culture.

To simply state that the Appalachian is like the nonwhite is to misrepresent and conflate very different histories and to undermine distinct lived experiences in a culture that privileges whiteness. My purpose is not to deny the power granted by whiteness but to complicate the ways that race and class are understood and represented. My purpose here is not to align with (and thus diminish) nonwhites, as if to say, "See, we are stereotyped, too. We might even have it worse than you." I do not believe that to be true. My purpose, rather, is to overlay multiple markers of identity so that a thoughtful onlooker might see that white privilege exists and extends into Appalachia but can also understand that the systematic representation of Appalachian figures has a precedent in the depiction of nonwhite Americans, with a similar investment in preservation of the normative. The simultaneous expectations of monolithic whiteness and portended denial of white privilege results in a figure that is at times shown as "pure Anglo Saxon stock" and at other times as "peculiar." This places an investment in whiteness and an investment in normative culture in conflict. The effect is a set of characteristics and stereotypes working both to romanticize and demonize a place. What is consistent in film and media is the need to show Appalachia as the other, to solidify the position of self.

My theorizing of the self-other split as central to the development of active subjectivity draws from Jacques Lacan's assertion that the split between *je* and *moi* sets into motion a desire for reconciliation. This process has been translated and is widely understood as the mirror stage.[17] On the application of Lacanian theory to film, Todd McGowan explains, "Traditional Lacanian film theory understands the gaze as it appears in the mirror stage and as it functions in the process of ideological interpellation. That is, the gaze represents a point of identification, an ideological operation in which the spectator invests her/himself in the filmic image" (2003, 27).[18]

Postcolonialism extends this subject-object relationship as it intersects with race and power. When Gayatri Spivak asks "Can the Subaltern Speak?," she is responding to conversations between Michel Foucault and Gilles Deleuze, bringing in readings of power and culture and representation from Louis Althusser and Karl Marx. Ultimately, Spivak concludes that the subaltern cannot speak. The broader conversation into which she enters asserts that the subaltern are, instead, silenced. The subaltern figure is represented by outsiders as an object for consumption. The effect of such representation and consumption of the represented is one-half of the equation. The role that the represented play to those normalized through such othering completes the equation and offers an answer to questions of motivation. In *Orientalism*, Edward Said not only is interested in the ways that the "Orient" is invented as a "place of romance, exotic beings, haunting memories and landscapes, remarkable experiences" (1978, 1) but also attends to the reciprocation of identity development. "European culture," Said writes, "gained in strength and identity by setting itself off against the Orient as a sort of surrogate and even underground self" (3). Drawing from Spivak and Said, I ask what is to be gained by showing Appalachia as perpetually backward? Why exoticize, diminish, romanticize, and demonize Appalachia? The answers are the same answers that Said finds in his work on the Orient—serving to hold up the authority of the dominant figure.

In *Imperial Leather* Anne McClintock urges her reader to complicate a binary way of understanding imperialism, in much the same way that I hope to avoid the same binaries that affect regional studies. She writes,

> In my view, imperialism emerged as a contradictory and ambiguous project, shaped as much by tensions within metropolitan policy and conflicts within colonial administrations—at best, ad hoc and opportunistic affairs—as by the varied cultures and circumstances into which colonials intruded and the conflicting responses and resistances with which they were met. For this reason, I remain unconvinced that the sanctioned binaries—colonizer-colonized, self-other, dominance-resistance, metropolis-colony, colonial-postcolonial—are adequate to the task of accounting for, let along strategically opposing, the tenacious legacies of imperialism. (1995, 15)

The "tenacious legacies of imperialism" that shape Appalachian studies are often reframed but can be understood in this same way of thinking. The indigenous response to colonizing forces, most of which are fiscal rather than governmental, sets up a too-simple insider-outsider binary that I wish to complicate in my readings of representation of the region.

Cinema studies, like literary theory or cultural theory, comprises multiple theories that work to offer entry into a text. In cinema studies, however, the language of the gaze predominates even historicist and phenomenological approaches that emphasize the role of an audience as they watch—or gaze at—a screen. When spectators enter a dark theater, they are confronted with the imaginary. According to Lacanian film theorists, we enter into a relationship built on deception. Theorists explore the relationship between the imaginary and symbolic order; spectators rely on images that solidify the self-other relationship, helping them situate themselves in these terms. Simply put, we measure ourselves against the images that we see on the screen. Just as children look to the mother to learn how they are similar to and different from her to develop a sense of self, spectators are constantly repositioning themselves in relation to images on the screen. A young black girl who sees only Shirley Temple on the screen will have difficulty understanding herself in relation to these images, as Toni Morrison beautifully illustrates in *The Bluest Eye* (1994). Similarly, a young black boy who sees only servants and primitive Africans onscreen has difficulty understanding himself in relation to these images, as James Baldwin makes evident in *The Devil Finds Work* (1976). Appalachian children who see only negative images of themselves exoticized like *Nell* (1994; dir. Michael Apted) or romanticized like *Christy* (1994; dir. Patricia Green) will similarly have difficulty developing a healthy image of self.[19]

When Laura Mulvey's "Visual Pleasure and Narrative Cinema" (1975) draws attention to the "pleasure in looking," or what Freud calls "scopophilia," to explain the power dynamic of the gaze; she situated the power with the viewer who objectifies the (often female) bodies on the screen. Taking Mulvey's ideas further, bell hooks, in *Black Looks: Race and Representation* (1992) asserts that there is power in looking back. That assertion of subjectivity has a place as we look at the ways that Appalachia has been portrayed because, like black representations in hooks's analysis as well as in others, there is an active conversation about these images that complicates a complicit absorption of portrayals as truthful.

The question of power in representation became a central debate in the Frankfurt School, which emerged in the 1930s and evolved over the next three decades. With the rise in popularity and accessibility of television and film in the mid-twentieth century, theorists such as Max Horkheimer of the Frankfurt School, as well as the French theorist Louis Althusser, applied Marxist analyses of cultural production to the screens so many were turning toward. From Althusser's perspective, Marxist power remains with the producer of images—and more specifically with the system of production. The consumer of images, then, is aligned with the masses. The consumer not only is *not* in a scopophilic moment of pleasure while gazing at the screen but is rather a part of a system of reproduction of ideology. Althusser sees the viewers as interpolated into a role, passively responding and participating as the system of production intended. In this way of seeing film, not only is the object of the gaze pinned down and powerless, but the holder of the gaze, too, is futile to the power of the system of reproduction. Both are caught in a hegemonic relationship that depends on their participation, while convincing them of their desire to participate.

Reader-response theorists such as Jonathan Culler, Roland Barthes, and Stanley Fish explore the potential for consumers to interact meaningfully with and thus shift the purpose of texts. An optimistic reading of this consumption allows the spectator to not only look back at but also question and engage the objects on the screen. The viewer decides what to view and how to view it, participating (or not) in the capitalistic system of cinematic production.

From any of these vantage points in the discussion of power, production, and consumption, the figures portrayed—the objects—are powerless. The change that they make is due to the impact of the role that they must play. As I have written elsewhere, "Put within the context of racial production, both the consumer and the producer are situated within a racial hierarchy which privileges whiteness and depends upon blackness as its Other, and race itself is created in the exchange between the two entities" (2014, 288). When this frame is extended to Appalachia on film, the region itself is created in the exchange between consumer and producer. I am interested in the ways that cultural reproduction and its continuous consumption enforce a hierarchy that relies on the phenotypic whiteness of Appalachian figures but also represents them in ways similar to nonwhite figures. In other words, I am interested in investments in the unwhite.

In *Black Looks: Race and Representation* bell hooks writes,

> Without a way to name our pain, we are also without the words to articulate our pleasure. Indeed, a fundamental task of black critical thinkers has been the struggle to break with the hegemonic modes of seeing, thinking, and being that block our capacity to see ourselves oppositionally to imagine, describe, and invent ourselves in ways that are liberatory. Without this, how can we challenge and invite non-black allies and friends to dare to look at us differently, to dare to break their colonizing gaze? (1992, 2)

This call to first see ourselves as complex is the call that I echo to Appalachians reading this book. When we see the limits of representation, we must push back and name what is missing. We must complicate the image. We must claim subjectivity. This book proves that such an act requires might and clear intention. A transformation in understanding of Appalachia will not happen passively.

In his critical catalog of black stereotypes in film, *Toms, Coons, Mulattoes, Mammies, and Bucks*, Donald Bogle (2001) makes evident the functional use of a few types to represent African Americans in film.[20] In a discussion of each type, with examples ranging from silent film to 1990, Bogle demonstrates the investment in narrow definitions for the sake of ease and control. When a complex and evolving group of people is represented in a handful of caricatures, the depth and range of experiences is erased, and a rich woman becomes a dispensable housekeeper or a man with increasing power becomes a laughable coon.

The black-led movement for civil rights in the twentieth century, the American Indian Movement, and the Movimiento for Mexican American empowerment made way for a multiplicitous approach to and attack of misrepresentation of nonwhites in film and television. Similar to imaginings of nonwhite populations in America, Appalachia has become more of an imaged idea than an actual place. The scholarship on representations of Appalachia in general, and a smaller field focused on Appalachian film, can be enriched by screening films about Appalachia through the historical and theoretical lens that scholars have used to understand representations of nonwhites. Although each group is distinct in its history and positions of power, the use of narrowly defined images to control and distance a group is similarly active.

Scholars tend to talk about Appalachia as either an active subject or a passive object. To simply see cinematic images of Appalachia as the work of outside forces is easy. Compiling a list of stereotypes of the mountains is fairly manageable. That is part of what I have done here, offered in the appendix, continuing the work of Jerry Williamson (1994, 1995a, 1995b) and drawing on models in cinema and literary studies that draw conclusions from patterns of representation. I hope that I am doing more than this. Just as bell hooks calls her reader to "dare to break [the] colonizing gaze," in *Critical Regionalism* Douglass Reichert Powell calls us to see the dynamic relationship between subject and object (2007, 2). He writes, "When we talk about a region, we are talking not about a stable, boundaried, autonomous place but about a cultural history, the cumulative, generative effect of the interplay among the various, competing definitions of that region" (5). Powell continues, offering a clear model of scholarship that inspires my own: "Instead of asking whether a particular version of region is valid or invalid, authentic or not, this new regional scholarship asks whose interests are served by a given version of region. In short, the emphasis is not on what regions are but why they are that way, *on what they do as much as what has been done to them*" (7; emphasis mine). The challenge is to be able to hold the simultaneous truths of damning objectification as well as active participation in either affirming or resisting a role. Just as my map of Appalachia is a bit playful, so is the way that I try to enter this conversation. A movie can flirt with being subject and object, just as a place can be both Appalachian and not. For the purposes of this book, which aims to understand the ways that region invites racialized representations, the most clearly Appalachian texts are made central. *Deliverance* (1972; dir. John Boorman), *Cold Mountain* (2003; dir. Anthony Minghella), and *Medium Cool* (1969; dir. Haskell Wexler) each function as case studies to demonstrate unwhite Appalachia. *Deliverance* and *Cold Mountain* are clearly set in southern Appalachia (north Georgia and western North Carolina, respectively). *Medium Cool*, set in Chicago, includes Appalachian migrants who clearly identify with West Virginia. The primary texts, therefore, are the texts that most often come to mind when one thinks of Appalachia. I do, however, attempt to include other examples that are clearly set in the region—without offering here a complete catalog of Appalachian film. Appalachian films are rarely so specific as to allow me to draw my own map, county by county. When a county is named, it is almost always Harlan—and in these cases, few viewers will doubt whether the film is Appalachian. Most of the films discussed here are self-identifying Appalachian films. In any cases that the film's setting is questionable, I have attempted to explain my choice to include it. This book admittedly spends more time looking at what has been done to the mountains, but with a special attention to why. My final chapters work to show the ways that Appalachia represents itself, and invites more work in this area.

In *United States of Appalachia*, Jeff Biggers works to reverse the tendency of scholars to "dwell on what has been done to Appalachia, rather than what Appalachia has contributed to the world," demonstrating the impact that the region—or the idea of the region—has had on the shape of America (2006, xiv). *Unwhite* is interested in what representations of Appalachia do for the rest of the world but also what those representations have done to Appalachia. More than anything *Unwhite* explores the purposes of the images.

In certain circles the following joke used to circulate. Scholars of African American literature and culture Houston Baker and Henry Louis Gates Jr. are waiting for a cab outside of an academic conference, continuing their debate about race. Gates and Baker have been arguing about the social construction of race—Gates most adamantly against race as having a biological basis. Gates steps to the curb to hail an approaching cab, which passes them by. Another approaches and passes. Baker turns to Gates and says, "You still think race is a construct?" The point, of course, is that even if it is a social construct, it impacts the daily experience of the most educated, wealthiest, most privileged individual who is read as "black."

I situate my argument about region and race in the middle of this slippery mess—both acknowledging and leaning on the reality of racial hierarchies and white privilege, which extend to judgments about Appalachia, and also acknowledging the limits of such constructions and stereotypes. The maps and these various contradictory definitions of Appalachia are included here not to clarify once and for all what is Appalachia but to acknowledge their very messy nature. To make my way through this rough terrain, maintaining a position of both and resisting a step to either side and a slide into either dichotomous ravine, I not only loosely define the region but also depend on the definitions of others. I am diving into the conversations over culture industry and debates about whether the power to make meaning is with the producer or the consumer. Finally, I find myself laughing with Baker as cabs pass, stereotypes persist, capitalist oppression deepens, and definitions seem to stagnate. Yet . . . I remain playful with these terms in remembrance that race is relative and regional culture permeates across county lines. Importantly, the history of both nonwhite immigrants and slaves in America and the history of highlanders, hillbillies, and mountaineers have both been tied to a cycle of stereotypic misrepresentation and poverty. They can claim their region or deny it, but an onlooker interpolates them hillbillies, and the result is no different. By using the term "unwhite," I want to both assert that white privilege remains intact even in situations of poverty and exclusion and that the reliance on nonwhite tropes to depict Appalachia ultimately works to the detriment of Appalachia *and* maintains a white-nonwhite dichotomy to further privilege whiteness.

Chapter 1 ▸ Hillbilly as American Indian

"Paddle faster. I hear banjo music." Lately I notice this phrase printed on T-shirts and bumper stickers—the great markers of contemporary thought. As a native of the region in which *Deliverance* was filmed, and as one who has defended an Appalachian identity for as long as I've understood that I had one, these stickers confuse me. That they are sold at outdoor shops in southern Appalachia and stuck to pickup trucks and hybrids alike in the very region the stickers caricature, calls for an investigation of the rhetorical situation that has led to their popularity. A clear reference to the 1970 James Dickey novel and 1972 John Boorman adaptation, *Deliverance*, the bumper stickers recreate the semiotic problem of the film's reception. In the text and film banjo music and sexual assault belong to separate scenes and separate characters. The bumper-sticker phrase, though, is based on a conflation that erases one-half of the Appalachia that James Dickey and John Boorman convey in *Deliverance*—a damning and inaccurate synecdoche. The quaint and mythic genius of the young banjo player, representative of a traditional past both untouched by civilization and doomed to erasure, becomes conflated with the violence of two local men.[1] The bumper sticker demonstrates the misrepresentation of Appalachia in Hollywood cinema as unwhite—here marked, as Native Americans have been marked in texts since the earliest of American letters. Like the Native

Americans of James Fenimore Cooper's *The Last of the Mohicans* (2003), Appalachia represents not only the ambivalence around the quaint past that cannot survive the pending process of industrialism but also the inevitable violent brutality that emerges outside civilized reaches. The representation of Appalachia relies on a conflation of the myths of the "vanishing Indian" and the "civil savage," specifically as they were rendered in the 1992 film version of *The Last of the Mohicans*, directed by Michael Mann. To understand the treatment of the "hillbillies" in the popular novel and subsequent film version of James Dickey's 1970 *Deliverance*, and particularly to reckon with the characters who emerged from an arguably nuanced treatment into gross caricatures looming large in American sentiment, it proves useful to study the other through a racialized lens, understanding the ways that Appalachia serves to solidify the whiteness of the southern heroes.

▶ The Establishment of a Stereotype

With few words, and lasting only a few moments, a key scene in *Deliverance* establishes one of the most damning caricatures of Appalachia—the "monstrous mountaineer." The isolation of the hills leads to a depravity—often sexual in nature. Without the presence of a civilizing force, monstrous mountaineers are given reign to hone their self-serving cruelty. The pair of men who emerge from the woods in *Deliverance*, guns in hand, are the daguerreotype: physically repulsive, more animal than human, with overgrown hair and long utilitarian fingernails caked with dirt and oil. They are driven by desires—in *Deliverance* the desire is sexual, though in other iterations of the type the desire may be based on power, control, or greed. The monstrous mountaineer type, at least in *Deliverance*, is unwhite in that he exists apart from the white southerners, who are shocked to come across him, and because he has no access to the civilized white world that surrounds him at the foot of his hills.

The monstrous mountaineer can be communal or singular. In the communal monstrous form, the isolated victim is usually female and has been traumatized or threatened by her violent male community. The monstrous mountaineer takes the shape of the predominantly male community, while the narrative follows the victimized female. In several cases an outsider (male, and usually northern) helps the victim escape from the depravity of the mountains. *Winter People* (1989; dir. Ted Kotcheff) is a relatively contemporary example of this iteration. Set in the 1930s in a small North Carolina town, an outsider (Kurt Russell) rescues the heroin (Kelly McGillis) from her savage and isolated mountain community. The entire mountain region is monstrous, threatening the beautiful female lead until she is rescued by an outsider. Michael Apted's *Nell* (1994) similarly focuses on an isolated woman in the North Carolina mountains. As in *Winter People*, civilizing forces with the promise of romance (Liam Neeson) rescue Nell (Jodie Foster) from her isolation. Apted acknowledges with ambivalence the beauty and terror of Nell's position, holding outsiders accountable for some of her trauma. Nell is both monstrous in her savagery and beautiful in her navigation of that savagery. *Winter's Bone* (2010; dir. Debra Granik) centers around a young girl who is thrust into adulthood because of her family's involvement in the production and sale of crystal meth. Ree (Jennifer Lawrence) gains the empathy of viewers as she manages to survive in a dysfunctional, isolated mountain community. While there is abuse of power and cruelty and a ring-leader of the violent drug trade in the community, Granik resists the clear victim-perpetrator dichotomy and instead demonstrates the difficulty for Ree to ever leave her mountainous home.[2] In these and other films the isolation is at least partly to blame for the evils of the community. To enter unchartered space is to invite terror for the mountain folks. That terror of the unknown leads to the second genre featuring the monstrous mountaineer: horror films.

Less ambivalent treatments exist in the horror genre, which both precedes and follows Boorman's *Deliverance*. H. G. Lewis's *Two Thousand Maniacs* (1964) is an early slasher film set in an isolated southern community, in which a small southern town celebrates the bicentennial of a Civil War battle and exacts revenge on "Yankees" who visit for the celebration. A long list of films beginning in the 1970s is based on the similar concept of isolated mountaineers who attack intruders. Tobe Hooper's *Texas Chainsaw Massacre* (1974) and Wes Craven's *The Hills Have Eyes* (1977)—and to a lesser extent the Alexandre Aja remake of 2006—fit this general trend of isolation breeding violence, though neither of these films is set in the Appalachian Mountains.[3] Horror films set in Appalachia fitting the monstrous mountaineer type include Rob Schmidt's *Wrong Turn* (2003), Tony Giglio's *Timber Falls* (2007), and William Fruet's *Trapped* (1982). Set in West Virginia and Tennessee, these films fit into the "hixploitation" category, perhaps best exemplified in the 1987 comic horror, *Redneck Zombies* (dir. Pericles Lewnes). In each of these horror films, the caricature of the isolated mountaineer who turns to (sexual) violence and grotesque torture of outsiders or intruders can be traced to *Deliverance*.

The monstrous mountaineer type, solidified in *Deliverance*, is a predominant figure in the caricatures of the region. Though other types exist, the monstrous mountaineer is arguably the most prevalent. Geographic isolation, inbreeding and the resultant genetic deficiencies, and cultural hatred of outsiders combine in the stereotype most often associated with *Deliverance*.

▶ The Civil Savage and Vanishing Indian

In *Deliverance* the Appalachian figures are made unwhite and presented as parallel to Native Americans. Whereas Frederick Jameson calls *Deliverance*'s "hillbilly figures" a "disguise and a displacement" for "the peoples of the third World, of the Blacks, of the intransigent and disaffected youth" (1994, 57), I would argue that their typing is more aligned with the American Indians of the twentieth century, particularly in fiction and film. Two types—the vanishing Indian and the civil savage—function similarly in *The Last of the Mohicans* and *Deliverance*.

Ambivalent treatment of Native Americans in American literature, American popular culture, and Hollywood film has reflected the broader American sentiment. As D. H. Lawrence wrote in his 1923 *Studies in Classic American Literature*, Euro-Americans (whom he simply calls "Americans") have a "dual feeling" about the American Indian: "the desire to extirpate [him]. And the contradictory desire to glorify him" (qtd. in Deloria 1998, 7). As Philip Deloria puts it in *Playing Indian*, "Whereas Euro-Americans had imprisoned themselves in the logical mind and the social order, Indians represented instinct and freedom. . . . Savage Indians served Americans as oppositional figures against whom one might imagine a civilized national Self. Coded as freedom, however, wild Indianness proved equally attractive, setting up a 'havethecakeand-eatittoo' dialectic of simultaneous desire and repulsion" (1998, 2). Not knowing quite how to make sense of Indians as a part of America's evolving identity, most white Americans vacillate between romanticizing and demonizing them.

Since European immigrants arrived in the Americas, there has been a tense duality in white descriptions of Indians.[4] At the turn of the twentieth century "Indian" camps sprang up across the country, coinciding with Daniel Beard's development of the Boy Scouts of America and G. Stanley Hall's diagnosis of neurasthenia. The fear of overcivilization, embodied by Teddy Roosevelt, who would transform his image from a New England dandy into a "Rough Rider," led to a national movement to encourage young boys to return to the wilderness by "playing Indian."[5] In this iteration Indians are immune to civilization and provide a model for white boys—so long as the boys return to civilization after their summer at camp or their journey into the (already closed and thus imaginary) frontier. In the latter half of the twentieth century, the men's movement and the New Age movement borrowed heavily from an imagined Native American tradition, again engaging with the stereotype of the vanishing Indian. Here, Indians are romanticized as deeply spiritual and intuitive conservationists. Each of these movements, whether tapping into the Indians' savagery or spirituality, hinges on white performance of white imagining of Native American culture to preserve and improve white society. This long-standing tradition is based on the assumption that the white individual, who is almost always male, returns to civilization after his foray into the wilderness. Too much wilderness, it is understood, is destructive. Too much wilderness is what makes the Indians, ultimately, savage.

Hollywood film has both reflected and influenced this (mis)understanding of Native Americans, resulting in stereotypes that avoid an engagement with the long-standing ambivalent perception. Film- and ethnicity-studies scholars have documented the ways that filmmakers have played on and reiterated the stereotypes of Native Americans (see Bataille and Silet 1980; Churchill 1992; Friar and Friar 1972; Hilger 1986; and O'Connor 1980). Two key types, which are related to and drawn from this history outlined here, are the vanishing Indian and the civil savage, which simultaneously romanticize the Indian while acknowledging his imminent demise. The vanishing Indian myth is based on the idea that the culture of the Indian—with its lack of civility—is doomed to extinction. Supported by pseudoscientific evolutionary theory, which presumes the superiority of Euro-Americans, the inevitable disappearance of the Indian could be superficially mourned by a film's audience. Similarly, the type of the civil savage—an Indian who can, to an extent, keep his innate animalism in check to be a part of the obviously preferred white civilization—is built on similar prejudice. The civility is never to be trusted, while the savagery is both feared and revered. As Gregory S. Jay explains in "'White Man's Book No Good': D. W. Griffith and the American Indian," early films like Griffith's "depict the Indian as incapable of 'civilization' and predisposed to savage regression" (2000, 4).

▶ The Three-Tier System

Resisting the types that would become so prevalent in Westerns of the next century, James Fenimore Cooper goes to great lengths in *The Last of the*

Mohicans to avoid demonizing American Indians while praising Europeans. Terence Martin, in his discussion of Cooper's novel, asserts, "*The Last of the Mohicans* is thus a novel with three kinds of protagonist, one savage, one civilized, one standing between" (1969, 226). Similarly, Juliet Shields sees the male characters "along a gendered continuum of national identities that runs from brutish masculinity to overcivilized effeminacy" (2009, 140). In an article that focuses on the power of landscape and nature in *The Last of the Mohicans*, Michael D. Butler writes, "At the top of Nature's hierarchy, as delineated in *The Last of the Mohicans*, sits the rational white man; on the bottom the 'sagacious' beaver, a being whose 'admirable structures' lead Duncan to conclude that 'the brutes of these vast wilds were possessed of an instinct nearly commensurate with his own reason.' . . . Standing between them is the Indian, whom both Cooper and his characters often think of more as animal than man" (1976, 135). Each of these scholars explores the tensions between civilization and wilderness central to my own understanding of this world as a model for *Deliverance*. Rather than three kinds of protagonists, I assert that there is a clear protagonist and hero situated precisely in the middle of Shields's gendered continuum. Instead of the Indian in the middle of "Nature's hierarchy," it is the men who can pass from one world to the other—Hawkeye and Ed—who become heroic. Cooper sets up a three-tiered hierarchy—a dichotomy productive of an emergent ideal in the center. A strong dichotomy remains intact, but it is in the liminal spaces that our heroes emerge. The same "place of broken barriers where the boundaries between rational and irrational, natural and supernatural, seem to have given way" exists in *Deliverance* to simultaneously romanticize the wilderness and establish the dangers therein, producing a hero that navigates both worlds while firmly maintaining his own position of privilege (Butler 1976, 118–19).

The three-tier system in both *Deliverance* and *The Last of the Mohicans* is an extension of the dichotomies that define race relations.[6] At one extreme is the übercivilized force, shown as devoid of logical function or survival as well as morally unsound. Read as white as well as effeminate, this extreme in both texts is destructive to American masculinity. At the other extreme is the wilderness and those woven into the uncivilized world—read as unwhite or "red." There is, in both *Deliverance* and *The Last of the Mohicans*, a tentative appreciation for the mythic quaintness of the wilderness inhabitants as well as a glorification of the virgin land itself. Clearly, though, the wilderness breeds savagery and cannot stand against the force of progress. The protagonists, who are originally from the civilized side and thus retain their whiteness, have various levels of access to the untamed wilderness. In effect, a clear defining line between white and nonwhite has functioned as the basis of behavioral codes, cultural biases, de facto expectations, and laws. This line is blurred not only by the biological gradations between white and nonwhite but also by the behavioral associations connected to each.

The message in both *Deliverance* and *The Last of the Mohicans* is clear: white men playing Indian is understandable, but at the end of the day and the close of the wilderness—the flooding of the Cahulawassee or the close of the frontier—the rightful place is closer to civilization, among one's own people. If race is performative, can a white man act enough like an Indian to count as one? Similarly, if the line between urban and rural is as distinct as narrator Ed Gentry describes it being, can a city boy become a part of the wilderness for a long weekend? The answer each time is both yes and no. Hawkeye, a "white" man raised by Mohicans, has knowledge of and access to Indian culture. Ultimately, though, at the death of his "brother," a true Mohican, Hawkeye's adopted father acknowledges the limits of Hawkeye's claims of Mohican blood. His white ancestry keeps him from being truly Mohican. From the perspective of a white reader or viewer, this liminality is ideal. He has been able to play Indian but can walk away with the "white" British daughter to their own frontier, white privilege intact.[7]

In *Deliverance*, the Atlantans consciously play Indian, illuminating the three-tiered hierarchy. Expressed even more clearly in Dickey's novel, each man acknowledges the rejuvenation of escaping the city using language of Indian performativity. When Ed hunts, he says, "hunting and pretending to hunt had come together" (1970, 95).[8] Ed acknowledges directly that in lieu of experience, cultural images teach him how to paddle: "Movies and pictures of Indians on calendars gave me a general idea of what to do" (72). He and his friends can play Indian, although finally the wilderness in the form of the river and of the untamed people shows the Atlantans they are outsiders. One man is killed, one is disfigured, one is raped, and all are transformed. The character who survives this expedition best, Ed Gentry, proves that—like Cooper's Hawkeye—he can access the wilderness with some level of legitimacy but ultimately belongs back in his rightful place among the civilized. Racially, the protagonists maintain white privilege. Hawkeye marries and leaves for the white man's frontier. Ed returns to Atlanta and the world of advertising. They are white in opposition to the nonwhite Indians and the unwhite Appalachians, respectively.

► Overcivilized Whites as Weak

At one extreme of the three-tiered hierarchy, in both *Deliverance* and *The Last of the Mohicans*, is the weak whiteness of overcivilization as represented by conceptual Atlanta and Europe and embodied by the characters of Bobby and Duncan, respectively. In both works the "homeland" is a place both imprisoning and validating. Civilization, which is too limiting to heroic Ed and Hawkeye, defines the unquestioning figures of Bobby and Duncan.

In *The Last of the Mohicans*, as presented by Michael Mann, Europeans are represented as untrustworthy, ineffective, and effeminate. While Cooper's novel distinguishes between the French and British leaders, Mann's cinematography and editing conflates the two, particularly in darkened battle scenes between faceless soldiers who adhere to the rules of engagement. The depiction of the three military leaders, General Webb, Colonel Munro, and General Montcalm, positions them as similarly untrustworthy.[9] Each of these representations of civilization is weakened—morally and physically—by their order. Their fighting is shown to be meaningless and ineffective, from large battle scenes outside of Fort William Henry to the futile defense against the Huron attack, as commanders in powdered wigs and uniforms fight savage brutality with order and control—and lose.

The most literal embodiment of European civilization and its effeminate weakness in *The Last of the Mohicans* is Duncan Heyward. The casting of Duncan as red-haired and freckled Steven Waddington offers stark physical contrast to the darkness of his double-foil, the biologically white but culturally Indian Hawkeye, played by Daniel Day-Lewis. Duncan is the perennial suitor of Cora, the eldest daughter of Colonel Munro. Moments throughout the film characterize Duncan as dishonest and incapable of survival without the assistance of the Mohicans like Hawkeye.[10] Throughout the film Duncan remains a relatively shallow character, embodying the weaker, whiter, more civilized alternative to the heroic Hawkeye.

Like Mann's America, the Atlanta of *Deliverance* never feels like an actual place but is instead a representation of civilization and the loss of individual wilderness. An imprisoning suburban expanse, the city is defined by consumption and advertising devoid of meaningful exchange. In Dickey's novel, much more time is given to protagonist Ed's reckoning with his career in advertising, while Boorman condenses pages of this theme into the voiceover that opens the film. Through dialogue, delivered as voiceover while a slow pan shows the energy plant preparing for the pending flood, four indistinguishable voices belonging to the primary characters discuss a plan to raft the Cahulawassee before it is dammed. The effect of voiceover is a homogenization of the city boys as outsiders coming into an area that is, as is conveyed visually, being controlled by corporations and spoiled by man. While we later learn of the differences among these four men, they are initially—through blind voiceover—established as on one side of a dichotomy.

Aligned with Duncan in *The Last of the Mohicans*, Bobby is most effeminate and linked to (over)civilization, and, like Duncan, he is figuratively sacrificed at the hands of the savages. Bobby is played by Ned Beatty, with light red hair, freckles, and an extra thirty pounds. Bobby's softness is contrasted with the sculpted body and darkness of Lewis (Burt Reynolds) and to a lesser extent Ed (Jon Voigt). Bobby, who has been physically violated, becomes dependent on Ed's physicality for their survival. As the film progresses, Ed steps into the role of hero, encountering his inner primitivism. Bobby, on the other hand, shrinks into an infantile state of dependence.

Bobby's role as the weak civilized outsider is evident in several scenes, including an early scene in the film, when the four Atlantans arrive in Oree to fill their cars with gas and hire two men to drive their cars down to Aintry for their takeout on Sunday.[11] Camera angles privilege the Atlantans early in this scene, as they are focused in the foreground with the Appalachian figures in the background, creating a sense of both anonymity and homogeneity. As a cultural tourist, Bobby fails—in a Lacanian sense—to *see* the locals at all. Bobby is marked throughout the early film as an outsider without true appreciation for the wilderness or its inhabitants. After his first night in the woods, Bobby says, "I'm tired of this woods scene; I'm tired of shitting in a hole in the ground. This is for the Indians" (J. Dickey 1970, 100). Bobby, after all, "is unable to adapt to the system in which he finds himself and instead of 'shitting' in a hole . . . he soon finds his own inner space violently colonized, disrupted, and filled" (Clabough 2002, 43–44). Jameson's assertion that a "post-industrial America . . . gazes with fatal incomprehension at other cultures and, indeed, at its own past as well" characterizes Bobby's unwillingness to "shit in the woods" and arguably explains Dickey's choice to make him the victim of the pending sexual attack (1970, 56).

Vanishing Indians and Disappearing Hillbillies

At the other extreme of the spectrum are the locals who exist a world apart from civilization. Wilderness existence in America—whether Native American or

Appalachian—is dually represented, building on a long history of ambivalence. There is simultaneous praise for and condemnation of a more primitive way of life, creating one image of Native Americans and Appalachians that is a mythic remembrance of a past way of life and another image that is backward and repulsive. Both are present in the representations of Native American and local culture in *The Last of the Mohicans* and *Deliverance*. Borrowing from Native American studies and cinema studies, the "vanishing Indian" and the "civil savage" serve to make clear the connection between *Deliverance* and *The Last of the Mohicans*, while showing the social function of such types, perpetually setting the Native American and local as the other.

In the three Mohicans we see the ultimate—and perhaps the first literary model for—vanishing Indians. In the film's opening scene, a long shot follows Chingachgook, Uncas, and Hawkeye as they sprint through a deep and hilly forest. They each bound beautifully and nearly silently in this scene that is dizzying—both cinematographically with low angles as Hawkeye leaps above the camera's eye and psychically because the audience does not yet know from what or toward what they are running. The intense green that fills the entire shot merges with the epic orchestral music to create a triumphant intensity that situates these three men as heroic and nearly superhuman.[12] After a several-minute scene, the three men finally kill the deer that they have been tracking, immediately gathering around the dying animal to thank and honor him as a fellow brother; this initial introduction to these Indians marks them as connected to the land both physically in their ability to traverse it with animal agility and spiritually as they treat the object of their hunt with respect. There is a mythic aura surrounding these three Mohicans, who seem to know intuitively how to survive and thrive in the natural environment.

The mythic nature of the Mohicans is established in the film in part by their silence. Amid verbose but inept military leaders, the stoic nature of the Mohicans offers an important contrast. Duncan refers to the Mohicans as scouts, to which Hawkeye replies, "I ain't your scout. And we ain't no damn militia." Similarly, the blocking of the scene that first contrasts the Mohicans with the British makes clear their separation. The Mohicans are physically kept apart from the British throughout the scene. This distancing, established in this and other scenes, privileges the Mohicans as outside of the realm of overcivilization. Specifically, the Mohicans as a group are situated as mythic and otherworldly as they flitter in and out of the scene as they desire, while the overcivilized are framed cinematically, as though they were trapped indoors.

The "disappearing hillbillies" qua vanishing Indians are first shown in *Deliverance* as spectral beings living outside the reaches of civilization. In the first Appalachian scene of *Deliverance*, early in the film, the Atlantans make their way to the small post of Oree, deep in the Appalachian hills, setting up a key treatment of the locals. As Daniel B. Marin points out, "In this boy, whom they meet before getting on the river, is a kind of preview of the river itself: crazy and wild, but beautiful too" (1970, 116). Lonnie, the banjo player, captures the quaint and mythic image of Appalachia like no one else in the film. Lonnie also represents the ambivalence of Appalachia, demonstrating "simultaneous couplings of attraction and revulsion" (Aigner 1972–73, 41).

The "crazy and wild, but beautiful too" aspect of Lonnie and Appalachia in general seems to have become synonymous with the riff from the Dueling Banjos as well as becoming conflated with the threat of violence from within the region. At its core, though, the depiction of Lonnie, as he engages with Drew Ballinger in a guitar-banjo duel, reveals the ambivalent respect for and repulsion by the isolated idiot savant. Lonnie's distant stare, his odd physical appearance (created in part because the arms that we see playing the banjo are not actually his), and the cinematographic choices heighten the gap between the Atlantans and the locals, while also providing a crossroad in which they might actually communicate. The communication, however, is aborted by Lonnie's sensibilities as well as Bobby's judgments.

Boorman uses camera angles, diegetic sound, and quick editing to establish the tentative but ultimately commercial relationship between the white outsiders and the unwhite locals who are, in this scene, quaint and odd. As Drew, a genuinely interested and unbiased lover of music, begins to play with Lonnie, the "ding" of the gas pump creates a trio—a symbolic creole language of trade and commerce that brings these two peoples together. As the two trade phrases, a connection is made, and the gas pump fades away. The duel has begun.

Drew is shown to be inferior through his less impressive picking, but also through the high angle that Boorman uses to shoot him. Lonnie, on the other hand, is shot at an extreme low angle, creating a sense of authority that adds to his ability on the banjo. Close-ups of facial expressions—memorably of Lonnie's grin—combine with long-distance reaction shots of the other Atlantans and the locals. A bewildered Drew invites him to play another and is dismissed squarely as the fleeting moment of connection passes and the curious locals become distant and threatening. The line between civilization and wilderness is clearly drawn by the scene's end, leaving a haunting image of the mythic genius of the mountain boy.

▶ Civil Savage and Monstrous Mountaineer

To maintain white civilized normativity and to justify the eradication of Native American cultures filmmakers call on the "civil-savage" iconography. This type proves that the innate savagery of the Indian emerges eventually, even when educated, entrusted, and enculturated. To offer the balanced characters of Hawkeye and Ed, and especially to justify the destruction of a region and the end of a culture, the negative extremes of the wilderness must be demonstrated. Neither Mann nor Boorman shy from conveying the terror and savagery of the wilderness. Both directors simplify novels that are more nuanced, constructing clear antagonists that help justify the white man's treatment of the other.

The portrayal of Indians is among the most dramatic shifts—from complex to dichotomous—between Cooper's novel and Mann's film version of *The Last of the Mohicans*. In his novel Cooper works to complicate the perception of Indians by creating characters from various tribes, with varying degrees of civilized behavior. Importantly, individual characters, regardless of race or ethnicity, are developed fully enough that we understand their weaknesses, strengths, motivations, and desires. Maqua's brutality has more of a historical context in the novel than is allowed in the film, for example. Mann's film, though, relies on reductive associations between tribe and behavior. The Mohicans are thus represented as "good Indians," capable of civility, motivated by a love of the land, though ever capable of effective and vicious savagery. In Mann's telling of *The Last of the Mohicans*, the Mohawks juxtapose the Mohicans, representing the barely contained savagery that justifies the end of the Indian era that the film captures.

In *The Last of the Mohicans*, the scene of the Mohawk ambush on the British offers the most extreme example of Indian savagery in the film, especially as it is contrasted with the ineffectual civility of the British. After the British have very formally surrendered to the French, they find themselves in between two ridges filled with blood-thirsty savage Indians. Mann films this scene with sweeping shots of the bloodbath, punctuated by close-ups of particularly brutal moments of attack, like scalpings, the crushing of infant heads, and other especially brutal or bloody deaths.

The civilization spectrum is shown in this scene to demonstrate the futility of the British forces and the brutal violence of the Mohawks and to set up the intermediary effectiveness and heroism of the Mohicans—particularly Hawkeye. The British, already in retreat, maintain dignity through a pageantry of power. Their wigs, their uniforms, and their reliance on orders from superiors all function to weaken them in this attack by the Mohawks. While Duncan calls out firing orders, his ranks suffer torturous deaths at the hands of the Mohawks. Duncan is shown as not only unprepared to defend but fearful in a moment of actual confrontation. At the other extreme, the costuming of the Mohawks only adds to their endeavor. They are nearly naked, unencumbered by uniforms but painted for war, which adds to their terrifying presence and establishes unity. Their war cries seem to come from a deep animal place, in contrast to Duncan's superficial and heady firing orders. In one of the most brutal moments of this ambush scene, Maqua enacts a very personal and vicious revenge on "Gray Hair," shooting him and then pulling out his still-beating heart.[13] The individualized brutality of that death marks Maqua's savagery. The Mohicans emerge as the heroes of the scene, killing only when necessary, to save the Munro daughters. Hawkeye manages to beautifully leap through the massacre, efficiently killing when attacked, to reach Alice and Cora and lead them to safety. With more effective access to savagery than Duncan, but more civil rules of war than Maqua, Hawkeye strikes an ideal balance in this scene.

The action of *Deliverance*, in its film version much more than in the novel, characterizes the locals in two distinct categories, defined by two interactions. The first aforementioned scene in which Lonnie plays the banjo offers one view of the locals as disappearing hillbillies. The second and most infamous scene of the film, the rape scene, portrays the locals as monstrous mountaineers. This simplification of the region is reminiscent of Mann's portrayal of Indians. Even the quaint locals are innately untrustworthy and potentially dangerous, and the savage locals are savage in the most brutal way.

Boorman takes a horrifying scene from the novel and somehow transforms it into the defining moment of the film—establishing the brutal savagery of two men, which by extension came to characterize a region. James Dickey's son, Christopher, who worked as a body double for Ned Beatty during the summer of filming *Deliverance*, reflected on the transformation of the rape scene from novel to film:

I understood that was the way it was supposed to work. But I didn't think my father understood what had happened that day filming by the river. In the book you can read the rape scene and know it happened, but you get around it and go on, and get other things out of the novel. In the movie—it was becoming what the movie was about, it was the thing everybody was going to remember. "Squeal like a pig!" Not Lewis's survivalism, not the climb up the cliff, not Ed's conquest of his own fear. It was all going to be about butt-fucking. (1999, 180)

The audience's visceral reaction to the rape scene, which Christopher Dickey aptly characterizes as disproportionately memorable, results in a simplified stereotypic image of Appalachia. The monstrous mountaineer becomes a villain, justifying his murder and the destruction of his home.

Boorman uses framing, camera angles, and camera distance in two important scenes to establish power dynamics. When the four Atlantans first encounter locals at a gas station, Lewis and Ed are emphasized in a medium-close shot, with one of the Griner brothers framed between them in the background. The effect of the shot is to show Griner as trapped by Lewis and Ed, who maintain control of the narrative of this scene despite their outsider status and their dependence on the locals for a ride. The next interaction with locals relies on the same framing, though the characters who are empowered are reversed this time. In the rape scene, Boorman emphasizes the two nameless men through a medium-close shot, with Bobby and Ed trapped in the background between them in the shot.[14] As the tension of the rape scene heightens, camera angles demonstrate to viewers the power dynamics. Bobby, the rape victim, is shot at a high-angle which makes him appear weak and vulnerable, while the two perpetrators are shot at extreme low angles, which makes them appear monstrous and empowered.

More than any cinematic techniques, of course, it is the plot of the scene in the woods that solidifies the reputation of these two men as savage and the city boys as overcivilized victims. As the locals turn this encounter into a forced sexual assault, planning to take turns with the two men, the action itself evokes fear from viewers. Bobby's role as overcivilized and effeminate is carried to an extreme as he is raped anally. Both the novel and the film, to varying degrees, suggest Bobby's passivity in the scene. Bobby is unable to resist this terribly violent and degrading period in which he is bestialized and effeminized, made to enact the fantasies of the mountain man. What is implied, though, is that this would not have happened to Lewis and did not, in fact, happen to Ed. Their own positions in the continuum between civil and savage seem to determine their masculinity and, in effect, their vulnerability to anal rape.[15]

The savagery of the mountain men in this scene, beyond the terrifying plot structure, is strengthened through a reliance on and combination of preexisting stereotypes of rural southerners. Frederick Jameson writes, "The new characters suggest a combination of hillbilly inbreeding and degeneracy on the one hand and the most proverbial barnyard perversion on the other" (1994, 56). These men are dressed in filthy, worn clothing, which, along with the lack of dental hygiene, suggests their poverty and isolation.[16] The dirtiness of these two men is captured in costuming, from their blackened fingernails to their greasy hair. That the first sexual encounter forces Bobby to "squeal like a pig" while the mountain man rides him, laughing and slapping him as a form of foreplay, supports the stereotype of rural southern bestiality. The broken diction; the seeming lack of intelligence, particularly in the second mountain man; and the allusion to a moonshine still are all based on well-established southern stereotypes. The sexualized savagery of the monstrous mountaineer must be controlled, even at the cost of the quaintness and the loss of culture.

Importantly, neither Boorman nor Mann is attempting to let two men or even one tribe represent Appalachia or Native Americans, respectively. Their films do, however, demonstrate a level of savagery even in the most civilized moral spaces, implying that the native culture (whether Indian or Appalachian) is too remote to be civilized. In *The Last of the Mohicans*, Mann goes to great lengths to portray the village life of the Huron tribe, with whom Magua has superficially aligned himself. We see villagers producing traditional wares, while women and children interact joyfully. Elaborate sets show the customs, housing, government, and dress of the Huron as historically grounded and civilized. Even here, though, the sachem demonstrates the potential savagery even in the most civil setting. Hawkeye reasons with the sachem in a very structured way, asking, "Would the Huron have greed for more land than man can use? . . . Would the Huron kill every man, woman, and child of their enemy?" Here, Hawkeye points to the different types of savagery of the civilized (greed) and the savage (sweeping violence). The sachem responds, "The white man came and night entered our future with him. Our council has asked the question since I was a boy: What are the Huron to do?" Ultimately, though, the answer involves a forced marriage and a sacrificial live burning. Even in a civilized fashion, the answers are savage.

In *Deliverance* what is presumed to be civilized and orderly—the police force—is found to have savage elements. The sheriff is constructed as intelligent and civilized but rough around the edges, instilling fear in Bobby and

Ed as they work to cover up their murderous "vacation" on the river.[17] The sheriff, however, is more Deep South than Appalachian in his drawl and slow manner. One deputy, Officer Queen, is a local man whose brother-in-law has gone missing. Queen's treatment of the men and the elevation of his personal concerns above the law begin to show the cracks in the police system. Further, much of the justification for the cover-up was based on the perceived injustice that would come from a local trial. As Lewis says, "All these people are related," to convince the other three men of the risks of letting this accident go to trial. By extension Lewis is condemning the entire region, presuming corruptibility.

Emerging from the opposite spectrums of these three tiers, with extreme civilization and extreme wilderness at either end, is a heroic intermediary white position. Embodied by Hawkeye and Ed respectively, this tier has access to Native American or Appalachian skills, an understanding of the powerful natural surroundings, and enough wilderness within them to survive. Importantly, though, both of these figures belong to the civilized white world and are finally able to create a productive merging of the extremes. This is what Jameson calls "some newer generation of more human and less legendary heroes" in his discussion of *Deliverance* (1994, 55). While this may be true, I would argue that the heroes in both texts are less legendary than some but are also specifically American in their merging of the wilderness and civilization. Diane Price Herndl argues that more than Cooper's novel, Mann's film situates Hawkeye as the ideal American in his liminal position: "'Hawkeye' shows himself, then, to be more aware of Indian values than the Indians, more condemnatory of the Europeans than those who have suffered most under the Europeans, and above all an American who is thereby not implicated in European greed, colonization, and racial slaughter" (2001, 268). In a parallel way *Deliverance*'s Ed Gentry is both civilized and animalistic in a way that he learns to harness. As Marin points out, "an animal of savage cunning that Ed hasn't known was there has thrust up from down inside him into consciousness and memory" (1970, 112). This inner animal surprises Ed as he carries out a calculated revenge, murdering a man presumed to be one of the rapists from earlier in the text. Importantly, though, he does not *become* an animal. Instead, he accesses his animalism while maintaining and returning to his position in urban Atlanta. Making clear that Ed is still civilized, Henry Lindborg writes, "The power with which his hero has been in contact makes him physically indifferent to his enemy and even to his own body, but it does not make him savage" (1974, 89). Whether it is merely a "temporary physical mastery over the environment" (Van Ness 1993) or if Ed "is able to transcend the restricted bonds of his senses" through the "ritual of the hunt" (Butts 1979, 49) is unclear. What enables him to survive, though, and leads him toward his ultimate transformation, is his access to both rural and urban knowledge. Both Hawkeye and Ed, as white American heroes, are able to condemn overcivilization, reify the threat of the wilderness, and retain the best of both worlds.

In the final scene of *The Last of the Mohicans*, immediately after the death of Uncas—the biological son of Chingachgook—Hawkeye's racial position is solidified through framing, editing, and dialogue. Hawkeye, raised by Chingachgook and alongside Uncas, is culturally Mohican. Mann's cinematography establishes Hawkeye's transition from Indian to white man in the film's final scene. At the scene's opening, atop a cliff overlooking the mountains, Cora is excluded from the frame, which focuses on Chingachgook and Hawkeye. As Hawkeye reckons with his father's dismissal of him as Mohican, the camera pulls back to include Cora. Hawkeye embraces Cora then, and it is Chingachgook who is excluded from the scene.

The camera holds Chingachgook in the foreground in a medium close-up as he says, "The frontier moves with the sun. Pushes the red man out of his wilderness forest. In front of it. Until one day, there will be nowhere left. Then our race will be no more or be not us." Hawkeye responds, "That is my father's sadness talking," as Cora remains framed as a part of the conversation. Chingachgook's response, along with the editing and framing, establishes the white intermediary position of Hawkeye. As he says, "No, it is true. The frontier place is for people like my white son and his woman and their children," Chingachgook, Hawkeye, and Cora form a diagonal, with Chingachgook in the foreground. As he continues, the camera angle shifts, filming the three characters from behind, against the mountainous landscape: "One day there will be no more frontier, then men like you will go, too. Like the Mohicans, new people will come, work, struggle. Some will make their life. But once, we were here." As Chingachgook states the film's final sentence, the camera frames Hawkeye aligned with Cora, with Chingachgook isolated at a distance, demonstrating Hawkeye's shift toward the civilized white world. His access to the Native American world has distinguished him from Europeans, though he is finally situated as the "white son" with rights to the land.

Deliverance's Ed Gentry occupies a comparably empowered position, as he accesses both the civilized and the wild. No one scene captures this liminality, though his otherworldly ability to climb a cliff while holding a bow and arrow, fatally shoot his target, and then repel back to relative safety—all while wounded in his side—demonstrates his functionality in the wild. That he devises their escape route not only through his intellect (thinking as he would, but also thinking as the monstrous mountaineer might) but *also* through his physical strength validates him as an occupant of both worlds. It is Ed who understands the merging of the two worlds that once seemed so distinct. As Peggy Goodman Endel explains, "That the opposites of the natural world interpenetrate is the final lesson of the river, and it is this rich principle of natural design which Dickey's narrator embraces at last as a principle of artistic design" (1994, 185).

Ed's position is most clear in contrast to the other Atlantans. Lewis is seemingly the most obvious hero, as the group sets out to the wilderness upon his suggestion and at his guidance. Lewis is extreme in his romantic view of the region, though. He commands the group as a leader but lacks the information and ability to lead them. The locals laugh at him, for instance, as he struggles to find a place to put the boats into the river.[18] Bobby's ineffectiveness is drawn from his overcivilization and fear of the wilderness. Drew, who respects the mountain culture and is cautiously skilled in navigating the river, remains bound by civilized codes of morality—codes that might lead to the death of more of the Atlantans if followed. It is Drew, the "industrialized everyman," who protests vehemently that they must report Bobby's attack and the shooting in self-defense to the police (Clabough 2002, 47). He is too much of another world to survive in this one. So it is Ed who knows enough of the wilderness to survive in it and enough of civilization to return to it.

Ultimately, both Hawkeye and Ed embody the redemptive qualities of both worlds. It is clear that the ways of the native and local culture will soon be lost, as foretold by Chingachgook and Georgia Power. One will be pushed west; the other will be flooded. To hold to the ways of the past would be futile and undesirable, while to be fully engulfed by civilization and its discontents would be foolish and weak. The unwhitening of Appalachia, like the stereotyping of the Native Americans, functions to preserve whiteness while maintaining an ambivalence about the clearly inferior racial other.

Chapter 2 ▶ Appalachian Woman as Mammy

The 1967 song "Rocky Top" paints a picture of a mythic mountain girl who is "half bear the other half cat." She is "wild as mink and sweet as soda pop," according to the song.[1] Her appeal is her balance of animalism and femininity, wildness and suppleness. "I still dream about that," the Osborne Brothers sing. This "Rocky Top" image makes evident the exoticizing of the mid-twentieth-century Appalachian woman reminiscent of the portrayals of women of color. In the Osborne Brothers' song the insinuation is that she belongs to the realm of dreams because she has not been completely tamed. Like the Anglo-American obsession with the nonwhite figure whose animalism and savagery legitimizes but also "ostracizes" him, the female iteration of the Appalachian woman is similarly marked as nonwhite. One Appalachian figure, Ruby Thewes of *Cold Mountain*, as embodied by Renée Zellweger, finds its closest model in *Gone with the Wind*, with Hattie McDaniel as Mammy. Both women play the role of the helpmate, drawing empathy from and alignment with general audiences, while remaining secondary to the plot of the white southern belles' often dramatic romantic plights. Both Mammy and Ruby are caricatured in positive and negative ways: these women have practical knowledge, they can survive through their own labor, and they are bold enough to stand up against social norms, yet they provide comic relief, lack the narrative opportunity for full development, and exist to further the plot for the primary characters. In each case, the Mammy-Ruby figure does help transform or at least educate the helpless white woman. This assistance continues to place her in a secondary role while the helpless heroine transforms into a more capable woman.

Like the mammy, who can be traced through two distinct lines, the Appalachian woman has both a passive drudge lineage and a spunky back-talking lineage. Both are grounded in knowledge of land, capable domesticity, and practical survivalism. The first is pitiable, while the second is laughable. Ruby Thewes, like Hattie McDaniel's mammy, brings together the two traditions into a more rich character but cannot escape the secondary nature of her role.

In the character of Ruby Thewes, the drudge is complicated, as was the mammy figure complicated in its later iterations. Frazier's Ruby is relatively complex, enabled to tell her own story and trusted to guide protagonist Ada out of despair. She is, I assert, an improvement on and an expansion of the drudge figure. Frazier's Ruby makes her own decisions—within limits—and is offered a fairly strong voice from which she expresses distaste, longing, gratitude, and tenderness. As Ruby appears in the 2003 film adaptation by Anthony Minghella, though, she has become a caricature that is perhaps better than the earliest outsider descriptions but less nuanced than her literary predecessor. Minghella's direction and Zellweger's embodiment of Ruby is reminiscent of the cantankerous but knowledgeable mammy figure as appears in the 1939 adaptation of *Gone with the Wind*.

Zellweger's Ruby Thewes borrows from two established Appalachian female types—the drudge and the feist—much in the way that Hattie McDaniel's mammy borrowed from two of the established black types—the mammy and the Sapphire. Both actors find space in the roles for subjectivity and agency, yet both are ultimately helpmates to the white southern belles that they serve.

Appalachian women have been depicted with more nuance by Appalachian writers such as Harriet Arnow and Wilma Dykeman. Shown as strong, confident, and independent, the women in their novels, like Arnow's *Dollmaker* (1954) and Dykeman's *The Tall Woman* (1962), had a ferocity and determination that harkens back to mountain women like Mary Harris Jones (Mother Jones), who organized women for the labor movement in the early twentieth century, or Ollie "Widow" Combs, who protested strip mining in 1965, resulting in legislation in the Kentucky General Assembly. Because filmmakers were uncertain how to understand women like Jones and Combs in cultures and periods that preferred women to be silent and dutiful, popular images of Appalachian women of this vein were caricatured in the form of women like Granny Clampett or were silenced through the lens of the outsider. In *Cold Mountain* Charles Frazier arguably continues the Arnow-Dykeman tradition of celebrating mountain women, in figures such as Mrs. Swanger and to some extent Ruby Thewes, yet the cinematic version of Ruby does more to reify the Hollywood and cartoon caricatures.

▶ The Mammy Type

Most often associated with the genre of postbellum plantation literature of the late nineteenth century, which celebrated the antebellum racial order, the figure of the mammy functioned to justify slavery, offer comic relief, and forward a narrative for white protagonists. Although it is not a part of the plantation movement and was written as an abolitionist text, the 1852 novel *Uncle Tom's Cabin* by Harriet Beecher Stowe establishes a central mammy figure in the character of Aunt Chloe:

> A round, black, shiny face is hers, so glossy as to suggest the idea that she might have been washed over with the whites of eggs, like one of her own tea rusks. Her whole plump countenance beams with satisfaction and contentment from under a well-starched checkered turban, bearing on it, however, if we must confess it, a little of that tinge of self-consciousness which becomes the first cook of the neighborhood, as Aunt Chloe was universally held and acknowledged to be. (1966, 31)

The mammy's "satisfaction and contentment" served Stowe's abolitionist purpose of ensuring that she was not perceived as a threat. As David Pilgrim, curator of the Jim Crow Museum of Racist Memorabilia at Ferris State University, explains, the mammy "spoke bastardized English; she did not care about her appearance. She was politically safe. She was culturally safe. She was, of course, a figment of the white imagination, a nostalgic yearning for a reality that never had been" (2012). Stowe imagines and represents a slave woman whose passivity and contentment demonstrates the possibility for liberation without threat of retaliation. Later, in the tumultuous years of Reconstruction, the mammy was refigured to exemplify the simpler times when everyone "knew his place."

The plantation myth depended on "happy darkies" who were content as slaves but were also dependent on whites as caretakers. While the height of this literature was in the late nineteenth century, assisting the erasure of newly granted rights for freedmen, the caricatures established in plantation literature made their way into the earliest films and have, arguably, never quite left.

Functionally, the mammy assures white readers or viewers that she is content and that white children are in good hands with her. Secondarily, the mammy is desexualized to make clear her nonthreatening position in a culture that depended on a disengagement with black-white sexual relations to maintain order. To acknowledge the systematic rape and abuse that black women suffered at the hands of white men was to make visible the tenuous system itself. The black woman who is maternal but not sexual, and knowledgeable but not threatening, keeps alive this construction and allows white readers and viewers to see the woman who is nursing a white baby as not fully human and thus not in need of full rights.

Despite the persistence of the mammy figure throughout the twentieth and into the twenty-first centuries, McDaniel's embodiment of Mammy in the 1939 film adaptation of *Gone with the Wind* stands as a turning point in the conception of the mammy. In *Toms, Coons, Mulattoes, Mammies, and Bucks*, Donald Bogle works to assert the complex nature of Hattie McDaniel's mammy role in *Gone with the Wind*. Although he calls her a "pre-Fellini-esque figure of the absurd," Bogle reads Mammy, as enacted by McDaniel, as empowered and independent (2001, 83).

Drawing from several studies of the mammy, which reach slightly different conclusions, I assert that we can understand the pre-McDaniel mammy in two veins, which McDaniel brought together to create a more empowered position. One vein has its roots in Harriet Beecher Stowe's mammy figure in her novel *Uncle Tom's Cabin*, and the other took shape in the 1914 short film produced by Sigmund Lubin, *Coon Town Suffragettes*.[2]

In a 1924 reflection on antebellum southern culture, Francis P. Gaines writes, "There can be no doubt that with the peculiar African capacity for devotion, the old mammy dearly loved her charges" (qtd. in Wallace-Sanders 2008, 8). To see this devotion as instinctive and even biological justified the continued white embrace of the figure. As Kenneth W. Goings points out in his analysis of black memorabilia, *Mammy and Uncle Mose: Black Collectibles and American Stereotyping*, these myths and stereotypes are born of the white imagination: "White Americans developed the stereotypes; white Americans produced the collectibles; and white American manufacturers and advertisers disseminated both the images and the objects to a white audience" (1994, xix). This model of white creation, white production, and white consumption is true of literary and cinematic stereotypes as well. In the early twentieth century, by the period of sound film, there was a paucity of black filmmakers and studios. The choices for black actors, therefore, were limited to the white imagination. The white imagination regarded the "best" blacks as loyal yet dependent, maternal yet masculine, industrious yet unambitious. In other words, the "best" blacks were never a threat to a racial order that privileged whites. The plantation-myth mammy fit this need and still retains its place in the twenty-first century.

A catalog of roles fits the plantation-myth mammy type, and a number of the early roles were played by Hattie McDaniel before she arguably constructed a melded mammy form. McDaniel played a mammy-like maid in her (uncredited) debut in *The Golden West* (Howard, 1932). Her roles became increasingly empowered, culminating in her embodiment of Mammy in the 1939 film *Gone with the Wind*. Following this role she had an active career but was typecast until her final role in the television show *Beulah* (1952). Scholars differ in their reading of her as Beulah or Aunt Tempy in *Song of the South* (1946); some read her as progressive in her back talk and sass, while others emphasize her narrow limitations to type.

A second inspiration for McDaniel's mammy is the Sapphire figure, which some parallel to the male Sambo or coon type. The Sapphire figure, like its male counter, is another iteration of invisibility. In her essay "Do You Remember Sapphire?" cited within "The Oppositional Gaze: Black Female Spectators," bell hooks writes, "Her black female image was not the body of desire. There was nothing to see. She was not us." Hooks recalls the Sapphire character from the television show *Amos and Andy*, and she recalls that as a child she saw Sapphire as a "bitch—nag" who was "there to soften images of black men, to make them seem vulnerable, easygoing, funny, and unthreatening to a white audience" (hooks 1996, 202). Sapphire is an antagonistic back talker, spunky and determined.

Contextualized among other black figures, and presented to a white audience, Sapphire, like Sambo and coon, is laughable. As the promise of Reconstruction came to a halt, the needs of a white southern audience shifted.[3] Whereas the violent brute slave captured the fear of whites to continue the enslavement of blacks, a postemancipation and post-Reconstruction audience tended toward a less threatening goof who needed white guidance. In reference to collectibles, Goings makes clear that during slavery there was no need for the sort of denigration that followed it (1994, xix). Nothing was more denigrating than the types that came to prominence like the Sambo and coon.[4] These figures, who are shown as "silly, stupid clowns, often afraid of the dark," reduce the threat of the black man. Donald Bogle supports this shift from D. W. Griffith's "villains" to the "black jester. High-stepping and high-falutin' and crazy as all get-out, the comic Negro was ushered in" (2001, 19–20). Hal Roach's young cast of *Our Gang/The Little Rascals* (1922–44) and holdovers from the blackface minstrels like Bert Williams exemplify this transition toward demeaning and emasculating humor, but nowhere is there a better example of the Sambo/coon figure than Stepin Fetchit, who "popularized the dim-witted, tongue-tied stammer and the phenomenal slow-lazyman shuffle" to the extent that "Negro bootblacks and bus boys were said to have imitated his notorious walk on the streets" (39).[5] Despite these demeaning performances, Fetchit, whose legal name was Lincoln Theodore Monroe Andrew Perry, was the first black to receive featured billing and would later assert his own role in carving out spaces for black performers after the civil rights–era critics dismissed his work completely.[6]

Hattie McDaniel played the coon-inspired mammy in many of her later works. She has been called the female Bert Williams as well as Eddie Rochester Anderson's female counterpart. *Judge Priest* (1934) featured both McDaniel and Fetchit in complementary but "niggerish" roles (Bogle 2001, 83). Pilgrim argues that McDaniel's began reshaping the mammy figure earlier: "However, her role in *Judge Priest* (Wurtzel & Ford, 1934) signaled the beginning of the sassy, quick-tempered mammies that she popularized. She played the saucy mammy in many movies, including, *Music Is Magic* (Stone & Marshall, 1935), *The Little Colonel* (DeSylva & Butler, 1935), *Alice Adams* (Berman & Stevens, 1935), *Saratoga* (Hyman & Conway, 1937), and *The Mad Miss Manton* (Wolfson & Jason, 1938)" (Pilgrim 2012). What McDaniel began in these films, she fully embodied in *Gone with the Wind*, alongside Vivien Leigh.

In *Clinging to Mammy: The Faithful Slave in Twentieth-Century America*, Micki McElya describes a mammy that is both loyal and crude, importantly pointing out her defeminization: "Their elaborate construction of the mammy included not only her physical attributes, which stressed her advanced age or wide girth, but also her spirited character. She loved her white 'family' and would defend and protect them fiercely, but she could be cantankerous with them and was a disciplinarian of white children. Mammy was endearing in her gruff demeanor and unrefined features, but she was the antithesis of desirable white femininity" (2007, 8). Literature had perhaps already allowed a blending of these types, but early twentieth-century film doubted an audience's ability to "read" subtlety on the screen and relied more heavily on caricature. For this reason it was not until 1939 that audiences saw a mammy who was neither silently loyal or ridiculously comic. Drawing consciously from both veins, Hattie McDaniel brings together the plantation-myth mammy and the coon mammy in her embodiment of Scarlett O'Hara's mammy in *Gone with the Wind* (1939). In her treatment of Hattie McDaniel's final scene of *Gone with the Wind*, Miriam Petty argues that McDaniel "performs her role with a degree of power and finesse that intersects with the myth of the mammy figure and the diegesis of *Gone with the Wind* itself to create a dynamic, medium-specific mammy monument" (2016, 29). McDaniel's active claim to agency offers a way of understanding the cinematic representation of *Cold Mountain*'s Ruby Thewes.

▶ Appalachian Women in Film

Despite the complexity of lived experiences, filmic representation of Appalachian women remains limited to a few stereotypes, which I call the *drudge*, the *feist*, the *granny*, and the *Mae*. Just as male stereotypes range from animalistic to civil, but are bound to a physical strength and knowledge of land, female stereotypes range on two axes. From drudge to feist, Appalachian women are shown in a range of passivity in which any action or selfhood is seen as a threat to the norm. Appalachian women also range from Mae to granny—with a tendency to portray Appalachian women at either age extreme.

Appalachian women in film often inhabit a secondary position—rarely heroic and typically disempowered. These women, young and old, inhabit the space of the other, even when they are the primary figures of a text. An active and clearly positive Norma Rae or a complicated but sympathetic Ree from *Winter's Bone* (2010; dir. Debra Granik) may find success or dignity in the realms in which they exist, but they are stripped of full access to female hero status in their portrayal. They may be beautiful—in their own ways—but they are not normative. They remain on the fringes of the American feminine. Like women of color, Appalachian women are reduced to narrow images—easily recognized and digested. In a few cases, on which I focus here, Appalachian women are given central positions. In nearly all these cases, though, the Appalachian female figure is drawn from recognizable stereotypes. More often, Appalachian women are secondary and serve to further the plot—much like Donald Bogle (2001) has asserted about African American women and Charles Ramírez Berg (2002) has written about Mexican

American women. The majority of Appalachian women in Hollywood film are images of the drudge or the feist and exist in either the very young and sexualized or the very old and asexual. Within these broader categories the feist is noted for being outspoken, direct, a bit wild, and acting outside the prescribed gender roles. The drudge inhabits the opposite behavioral space, quietly toiling, silently obeying, and drawing empathy without being fully developed into a character. Within these two larger categories can fit the subtypes of the Mae and the granny, differentiated by age as well as function for viewer.

In her review of Joyce Dyer's collection of Appalachian women writers, *Bloodroot*, Nancy Carol Joyner writes, "The twin stereotypes of Appalachian women—young, innocent, submissive, unlettered ingénue and old, feisty, crude, unlettered crone—were challenged long before Al Capp finished his cartoons of Daisy Mae and Mammy Yokum, but this volume gives lie to those notions that still breed condescension, discrimination, and neglect" (1999, 196). Historical and sociological studies make evident the complex role of women in the Appalachian region. The purpose here is to explore the trends and uses of images of Appalachian women.

Scholars before me have noted trends and patterns of representation of Appalachian women. Most notably, Sally Ward Maggard (1999) writes that there are four popular caricatures that linger and influence contemporary conceptions of Appalachian women, which she then narrows to two primary types, which I call the Maes (based on Daisy Mae and Ellie Mae) and the grannies (based on Granny Clampett and Mammy Yokum). The groups can effectively be split by age and sex appeal, creating the Daisy Mae/Ellie Mae/Daisy Duke group of young women who are beautiful, scantily clad, and have a varying degree of understanding of how to use their appeal to earn respect, which corresponds with their intelligence. The second group of elders—Granny Clampett and Mammy Yokum—are consistently unattractive and androgynous, with ranging levels of intelligence and respectability. I want to augment Maggard's character types, building on her useful analysis with historical representation of Appalachian women, drawn from literary depictions, journalism of the region, and documentaries of the "hillbilly."

I aim to take these primary caricatures and trends in representation and work to understand them in terms of power. Critical race theory illuminates these types, demonstrating that even primary Appalachian figures are shown as others—outside the expectations and behaviors of normative (middle-class, white, Christian, heterosexual) non-Appalachian women. According to Carol Mason, "By the time the word hillbilly first appeared in print in 1899 (Harkins 2004, 49), Appalachian men and women were well established as transgressors of modern, middle-class gender roles" (2009, 42). This depiction of Appalachians as transgressive threatens the maintenance of power. Whether the threat comes from a matriarchal strength with a refusal to cower in accord with gender norms or from a more passive ignorance of expectations, mountaineers that act outside of prescribed roles invite various forms of prohibition. One of the most effective means of controlling a people is controlling their image. Turning strength of character into caricature and making established traditions a punch line serves not only to entertain audiences but to weaken and control those represented.

The earliest cinematic representations relied on caricature to convey characteristics of the figures on the screen during the silent film era. In his important work *Southern Mountaineers in Silent Films*, Jerry Williamson (1994) offers an extensive catalog of films of the silent era that feature the mountain South. Summaries of films, which Williamson painstakingly crafted from screenings, reviews, and research on difficult-to-find reels, reveal a few key female tropes. In the 1910 film directed by Gaston Méliès, *A Mountain Wife*, the eponymous wife displays her wits in trapping an artist traveling with revenuers, her fierceness while driving him away at gunpoint, and her moral position of authority by leading her family into a new life on the right side of the law. This early image of "a mountain wife" plays to familiar remains of the cult of true womanhood but twists the image into a uniquely Appalachian combination of characteristics. She is not only morally correct; she is also fierce in her familial allegiance and unapologetically bold. These two predominant characteristics of loyalty and brash energy give way to two types that remain into the twenty-first century—the drudge and the feist.

Less a reaction to gender norms, the feist operates above gender norms in order to claim agency and maintain voice. The feist is typed to the figure that some have called the back-talking woman of Appalachia. This type appears less frequently in the works of people such as James Watt Raine and Emma Bell Miles for a few reasons. First, a back-talking woman does not deserve pity, and many early texts about the region were built on pathos. A reader of Mandel Sherman's *Hollow Folk* (1933) or Harry Caudill's *Night Comes to the Cumberlands* (1963) did not expect to see a fully realized woman. That image does not fit, which leads to the second reason that the strong woman is rarely shown in journalistic depictions filled with descriptions of the drudge: it does not serve the reader. With few exceptions writers who described the people of that Appalachian region were securely positioned outside of the region and were writing to an audience outside of that region as well. To romanticize life in the mountains in a simplified way allows the reader to pine for that life but understand the complexity and superiority of his position. To actually create full depictions of strong women who spoke up was not welcomed. Typified by figures like Norma Rae from the film of the same name or Ella Garth from *Wild River* (1960), these are women who take center stage and do not back down. The increase in popularity and representation of the back-talking woman corresponds both with a national distrust in government (post-Vietnam, post-Watergate) and with the second wave of the women's movement. In "'Beyond the Mountains': The Paradox of Women's Place in Appalachian History," Barbara Ellen Smith carefully describes the role of women. She points to what she calls "subterfuge" that talks back:

> Overt feminism was rarely the mode by which women on Big Ridge asserted themselves. Their tactics were often indirect, surreptitious, and on many occasions, humorous. Through her commerce and midwifery, Ellen Fridley [Smith's great-aunt] attained community visibility and social power, pushing against the constraints of womanhood in ways that conventional historiography would deem significant. But backstage, in a far less recognized arena, she also operated, using subterfuge and manipulation to contain the inequities of gender and set limits on male privilege, self-importance and authority. (1999, 12–13)

It is the "backstage" arena that arguably gets women like this represented as the drudge when she is actually closer to the back talker.

Certainly Kathy Kahn's study *Hillbilly Women* celebrates the back-talking woman. Aware of her cultural moment, Kahn criticizes the "media-created fads which advertise themselves as 'women's liberation'" and instead asserts that the women in her book belong to a larger and more legitimate movement. She writes, "Hillbilly women are real feminists; they have a history of fighting for the rights of working women in the Southern mountains. But they are also humanists. They are fighting for the liberation of all people" (1972, xxi). While Kahn gives women the opportunity to share their stories in their own voices, most filmmakers instead simplify complex women into caricatures. There are two resulting branches of this type: the young and sexy back-talking woman (one version of Maggard's Mae), who is likely to find love along with justice; and the elderly back-talking woman (one iteration of Maggard's granny), who is memorialized and linked to the past.

In "A Question of Loyalty: National and Regional Identity in Narratives of Appalachia," Mary Anglin discusses the back talking that went on in the mica industry in western North Carolina. She is interested in the conflict between the image of the region produced by local-color writers such as Mary Noailles Murfree and the stories told by the people themselves. In particular, she finds a contrast when in comes to loyalty. She writes, "Men and women alike 'backtalked' supervisors, left work to tend to farms and family matters, and used a rhetoric of reciprocity to make claims on those in charge." This image helps support the notion that the locals maintained a level of authority. Perhaps they did. Anglin is quick to note that "these rhetorical strategies did not so much destabilize the hierarchical relations of mica factories as they engaged a dispute over the meaning of authority. The history of unsuccessful efforts to unionize the mica industry may be viewed, at least partially, in this light" (1992, 105). Regardless of its effect on the mica industry, the concept of back talking as linked to authority and independence is central to the experience of some and the representation of an entire group.

▶ Appalachian Woman as Mammy

The figures of the drudge and the feist, discussed more fully in the appendix on cinematic stereotypes, merge in *Cold Mountain*. Just as Hattie McDaniel reimagines the mammy as she draws from the expectation of the traditional mammy, Renée Zellweger takes the traditional drudge figure and invigorates her with feist characteristics. Both are ultimately trapped in a performance of caricatures of their roles, yet manage some degree of autonomy.

In Anthony Minghella's production of *Cold Mountain*, Ruby Thewes's first scene immediately establishes her role in the film: she will provide comic relief, she will juxtapose the southern belle, and she will serve as secondary helpmate to protagonist Ada Monroe. Her practical abilities, presented in a forthcoming manner with little regard for etiquette, disarm and ultimately save a distraught and helpless Ada. Her delivery of this support presents a full and complex human being as a caricature of a mountain woman. Equally as important, this characterization also presents a sense of the place—Haywood County, North Carolina—in the figure of Ruby. Civil War–era Cold Mountain is shown to be a place that requires assertion, determination, and a bit of unbecoming behavior. If there is a face to this place, it is Ruby Thewes's. Nearly all that we need to know about Ruby is set up in her opening scene.

Ada Monroe, the Charleston implant who finds herself abandoned in Cold Mountain after her father's death, passively experiences the world around her. In Ruby's opening scene Ada sits writing in her deceased father's chair, rake propped beside her, as Ruby approaches boldly, saying, "Them cows wants milking. If that letter ain't urgent, is what I'm saying." She embodies a knowledgeable position, juxtaposing her own survivalist knowledge against Ada's "book smarts," which have left her hungry and hiding from a rooster. Ada has taken a completely passive position, finding no way to meet the challenges of the mountains. Exemplifying her fragility, an aggressive rooster is all but holding her prison on the porch. Ruby continues speaking to a stunned Ada, who has no context for a woman like Ruby. She curtly says, "Old Lady Swanger says you need some help. Here I am," making clear the role that she will play for Ada but demanding participation as she says, "And I'm not planning to work while you watch, neither." Interestingly, in the Charles Frazier novel, gender is acknowledged as a complicating factor of this exchange. In the book, Ada says, "I believe I need a man-hand for the job." An offended Ruby responds, "Number one . . . if you've got a horse I can plow all day. Number two, Old Lady Swanger told me your straits. Something for you to keep in mind would be that every man worth hiring is off and gone. It's a harsh truth, but that's mostly the way of things, even under favorable conditions" (1997, 67).

The screenplay maintains most of this conversation but leaves room for the threat that is more subtle in the book. In the film Ruby says, "Number two—there's no man better than me cause there's no man around who ain't old or full of mischief." What is established in both versions is Ruby's need for equal treatment and Ada's reliance on Ruby's survivalist skills. As the two complete their transaction and settle on the terms of their arrangement, the rooster catches their eye and draws the focus of the camera. Ada says, "There's a rooster—he's the devil himself," prompting Ruby toward one of the most memorable moments of the film, which confirms her practical approach, her comic role, and her complete juxtaposition to the Ada of this moment in the film. Ruby says, "I despise a flogging rooster" and promptly "picks up the bird and twists off its head." Turning to a shocked and gasping Ada, she says, dead rooster under her arm, "Let's put him in a pot."

In one short scene, Minghella has captured Charles Frazier's image of the mountain woman who arrives to save the southern belle and sets up the ways that the audience is to understand both characters. Through her knowledge of land, her pragmatism, and her nongendered survival skills, the mammy-helpmate saves the weak but beautiful woman while maintaining a secondary position. As in other depictions discussed in this study, the Appalachian figure—though phenotypically "white"—is stripped of white privilege and read as nonwhite in a racial dichotomy.

What is notable about McDaniel as Mammy, and what links her to Zellweger as Ruby, is the bold language and unwavering strength that each shows, even as they are bound as helpmates to another woman. The first image of Mammy in *Gone with the Wind* shows her to be in a slightly less empowered position than Ruby, which speaks to her status as a slave but also firmly establishes her fierceness. She is hardly the Aunt Chloe sort of mammy as she leans out of a window, yelling at Scarlett to remember her manners and wear a shawl. In this initial image Scarlett and Mammy are linked, and their early relationship is established. Scarlett ignores Mammy completely, unable to see how much she should actually heed her advice. Such are the first interactions between the two, before the war comes and Atlanta is burned. Mammy dresses, undresses, feeds, and scolds Scarlett. In return, Scarlett rolls her eyes, dismisses advice, rudely scoffs down food, and generally disrespects Mammy. In one scene Mammy encourages Scarlett to wear a shawl as she taunts the Tarleton twins, and Scarlett refuses. In another, prior to the picnic at the Twelve Oaks estate belonging to the family of Ashley Wilkes, Mammy demands that Scarlett eat breakfast, and Scarlett loses this battle.[7] Mammy makes evident that Scarlett needs tending, but Scarlett is still the center of the film and is, at this point, still our heroine—or as close to a heroine as she can be.

Both Mammy and Ruby shift into more central and empowered positions as circumstances around them force the southern belles to rely on their help. As Scarlett becomes more vulnerable with the loss of Ashley, the trauma of the siege on Atlanta, the death of her mother, and the insanity of her father, Mammy's figure shifts. Whereas earlier scenes place Mammy as a more comic figure who is an easily ignored voice of reason, she shifts into a more maternal figure after Scarlett returns to Tara. For the first time, Mammy looks to Scarlett for advice, asking what they should all do. Their relationship morphs, during the darkest times before Scarlett and Rhett are reunited, into one closer to collaborative. Scarlett understands all that Mammy knows about her. This mutual acknowledgement of Scarlett's ambition, at the expense of moral judgment, aligns them to work toward collective survival. Nothing signifies this more, perhaps, than the scene in which Scarlett rips down curtains and Mammy sews them into a dress. Two sets of skills and perspectives align under a common agenda: survival. Mammy knows better, and says so, but nevertheless helps Scarlett attempt to perform a social class that is no longer a legitimate fit for her.

For Ada and Ruby, a more genuine collaborative relationship develops quickly, as Ada is already in the throes of starvation and despair when Ruby enters her yard and wrings the neck of that "flogging rooster." In another early scene Ruby and Ada are at work mending a fence in the pasture, and Ruby is firmly in the role of teacher. Ruby quizzes Ada, asking, "What's this wood? . . . Where's north? Name me three herbs that grow wild on this farm." As they lift the logs to repair the split-log fence, a frustrated and exhausted Ada says, "I can't. I can't, alright? I can name the principal rivers in Europe, but don't ask me to name one stream in this county! I can embroider, but I can't darn. I can arrange cut flowers, but I can't grow them. If a thing has a function, if I might do something with it, then it wasn't considered suitable!" As Ada pitches this fit, throwing down her gloves dramatically and pacing through the field, Ruby remains calm. She looks on as Ada frets, and then calmly asks, "Why?" Ada explains that there is no answer and says that the fence that they are building might be the first thing that she's ever done that would produce an actual result. Ruby steps closer as Ada quiets and says, "So you never wrapped your legs around this Inman?"[8]

Ruby has the upper hand here, knowing all that is necessary for survival through the coming winter. She knows, too, that her role is not to chide Ada for what she does not know. Her final line of the scene positions the two women on a nearly equal level, as friends gossiping about men. Her interest in Ada's love life, though, reminds us of the central plot of the film and sets her in a secondary role, as a blushing Ada stomps off toward *her* house, with *her* virginity intact. As with Mammy and Scarlett, the work that Ruby and Ada do together is ultimately for the survival of the southern belle. That Mammy and Ruby have a roof over their heads is merely the salary earned for their work for the lady of the house.

As *Gone with the Wind* progresses, Mammy is allowed more frivolity and a small degree of sexuality as she wears a red garter that Rhett purchased for her. Even then, though, her sexuality exists to get a laugh. Mammy's subject position is a point of debate among scholars, and I assert that she does have a heightened degree of social status and personal autonomy as the film progresses but that she remains the secondary helpmate to Scarlett, who has become the villainous heroine by the end of the film. Mammy's feminine expression is limited to a garter. For both Mammy and Ruby, though, the clear sexual center is the protagonist. Each of these secondary embodiments of sexuality is meant to be somewhat laughable.

There is a tenderness to the love that develops between Ruby and Georgia (Jack White), a musician who travels with her father. As Ruby realizes her feelings about him, Ada understands and treats her as an equal by placing one of her own bracelets on Ruby's wrist. As Ruby, Ada, and the neighbor Mrs. Swanger walk home on Christmas night after an evening that included Georgia, Ruby talks about him in the disparaging way that a young girl might discuss her first crush. There is a moment that Ruby has a thing that Ada does not. Love and connection seem within her reach, while Ada's love feels distant and impossible. As the scene unfolds, though, Ada and Ruby are placed on equal ground. Ruby stops and asks Ada to name the constellations. It is a quiz that Ada passes easily, not because she has learned from Ruby but rather because it is a point of intersection between the applied knowledge of Ruby and the book smarts of Ada. Both women bring with them a knowledge of the stars, and both women are shown to be equals when it comes to love.

Not only does Ada depend on Ruby's approval—when Inman returns and expresses his desire to marry Ada, he asks Ruby's permission. He says, "I need your permission, Ruby, if I aim on living at Black Cove." Ruby resists any emotive scene and instead turns away, as she simply says, "Alright, then." Ruby and Ada are a part of something akin to a family by this moment and certainly by the end of the film. What they have endured has set them up to live out their lives together. With the end of the war in both films, Ruby and Mammy would be free to move on and establish their own lives independently. They do not, but instead remain loyal to the women whom they originally served.

Both the mammy and the helpmate roles dehumanized the woman whose complex position as caretaker and maternal guide continues to haunt generations to come. By the time that Hattie McDaniel came along and presented Scarlett O'Hara's mammy with a full complexity that was unprecedented, the concept of the mammy was already fully imprinted. Regardless of whether the *Gone with the Wind* mammy was new or simply the culmination of years of revising the mammy role, it is the *Gone with the Wind* mammy who is remembered as the mammy of the twentieth century. It is the McDaniel embodiment of the mammy, merging both the loyal and long-suffering mammy of the plantation myth with the cantankerous and humorous Sapphire, that offers a model for Ruby Thewes in the cinematic version of *Cold Mountain*.

Chapter 3 ▶ Mountain Migrant as Mexican Migrant

I n recent decades debates have emerged over the immigration of Mexican citizens to the United States. The word *immigration* brings to mind, for most Americans, questions over the Mexican-American border. As with stereotypes of other nondominant groups, the images of Latinos have shifted, following needs to portray them in a particular light. Legal battles, social trends, and educational policies have all influenced the experiences, as well as the images, of Latino Americans. As Western movies gained popularity in the 1960s, the Mexican figure was consistently present only to prop up the white hero. As relations shifted between the governments of the United States and Mexico, so did Hollywood portrayals. Since the 1855 Anti-Vagrancy Act was passed in California to prevent Mexicans miners from participation in the Gold Rush, the United States has continually crafted and revised anti-immigration bills aimed at preventing Mexican Americans from obtaining citizenship. This ostracism has been legalized at times, sometimes merely encouraged, but has consistently been supported by the Hollywood film industry. Major Latino stereotypes, including the "lazy Mexican," the "firecracker," and the "domestic," all work to set the Latino figure apart from the hero—as somehow outside of the norm. The investment in the Latino figure as the other remains consistent.

As I have worked to establish throughout *Unwhite*, the Appalachian figure has often been portrayed relying on established cinematic types. The experiences of urban Appalachians—mountain migrants who left the region for economic opportunities in the city—appear in film using the images, patterns, and rhetoric of films that depict Latino immigrants. Parallel patterns of in-and-out migration, maintenance of home culture, and a sense of threat from insiders marks the experiences of the urban Appalachian and the Latino migrant as similar. Two films, discussed further in the case study of this chapter, narrativize the experiences of these immigrants, making evident the role of assimilation and the threat of dominant culture.

Culture Shock and Imagined Communities

As Appalachian migrants left the mountains, many took with them a hope for a hasty return. Pushed out by a failing economy or a loss of industry and pulled away by the promise of new work and steady pay, mountain migrants felt tied to the mountains that remained behind them. Scholarship about Appalachian migration emphasizes not only the trends as families leave Appalachia, most often for urban employment, but also the return migration trends, which are highest in Appalachia (White 1989). Kathryn M. Borman and Phillip J. Obermiller (1994), Roger Guy (2007), and Susan Allyn Johnson (2000) have studied the communities that form among those who outmigrated from Appalachia. The general notion has been that urban Appalachians move, interact primarily with only the other Appalachian migrants that they meet, send their earnings back home or save to return home rather than invest in their new communities, and fail to assimilate.

The notion of failure of assimilation, shuttle migration, and the impermanence of Appalachian outmigration shows them to be outsiders who offer a slight threat to an established urban community. Rather than being brought into the fold, Appalachians have brought with them a strong sense of community that ties them to the mountains. Like contemporary arguments against Mexican American immigration, Appalachian migrants were seen as a threat as they formed communities among their own, worshipped in their traditional methods, and set themselves slightly apart. Scholarship and sentiment concur that mountain migrants tended to see relocation as a necessity that, if successful, was short-lived. This transitional and impermanent movement influenced both the experiences of the migrants and their reception in new cities. Not only did mountain migrants frequently feel unsettled in new cities, but they were often made to feel unwelcome. Patterns of shuttle migration established this sentiment, which is reflected in cinematic depictions of mountain migrants. On a larger scale these images of displaced and poorly adjusted mountaineers contribute to a swath of images of the Appalachian as other.

In 1940 sociologist J. B. Holt had developed what he called the culture-shock thesis, referring to the Appalachian migrant experience. Holt argued that the rise of Pentecostal religious bodies in midwestern urban areas was the result of the urban migration and urbanization of rural communities. Holt believed that the retention of culture, such as Pentacostal religious practices, reflected an inability to adjust, which he called "culture shock." Holt's thesis has been taken up and tested over the years and is worth considering and complicating if only because it served as a basis for the judgment of migratory Appalachians. Holt's focus on culture implies a stable dominant culture as well as, in this case, a stable Appalachian culture. In their 2016 article "The Uses and Misuses of Appalachian Culture," Obermiller and Michael Maloney call for a moratorium on the word *culture*. Holt's thesis serves as an example of the most outrageous abuses of culture, demonstrating a failure to join the new community because of an assumption about religious practices.

Holt's limitations point to a more useful framework to consider urban Appalachians, considering that representations of urban Appalachia have as much to do with the imagined Appalachia that protagonists leave behind as with the tactile Cincinnati or Chicago in which they find themselves. In his introduction to *Imagined Communities*, Benedict Anderson defines nation not by boundaries or legal allegiance but as an "imagined political community": "In an anthropological spirit, then, I propose the following definition of the nation: it is an imagined political community—and imagined as both inherently limited and sovereign" (1983, 5–6). One's alliance with a nation, or with a community, is not necessarily self-determined but is recognizable from within. No one can necessarily decide to be Appalachian, but those who are Appalachian are likely to feel a part of an imagined community, as Anderson describes: "It is *imagined* because even the members of the smallest nation will never know most of their fellow-members, meet them, or even hear of them, yet in the minds of each lives the image of their communion" (6). Anderson's concept allows for an extended definition of nation and of community, which applies to self-identified communities such as urban Appalachians. In the case of both Mexican American immigrants and mountain migrants, there is a static *place* from which these immigrants come. In their new spaces, however, they build a new hybrid community in what Gloria Anzaldúa (1987) calls "La Frontera." This liminal space, according to Anzaldúa, offers a productive "both/and" position, though, for some, liminality feels more like "neither/nor." It is the imagined community that marks these migrants as outside of the norm, experiencing liminality as neither/nor. This position places the concept of home in an even more haunting and encompassing presence, as they create a sense of longing for the places that they left out of necessity.

The perception of Holt's culture-shock thesis, combined with patterns of return and shuttle migration, gives locals in places like Chicago or Detroit the sense that mountain migrants are not only ill-adjusted to city life but that they are always already headed back "home" with no real desire to acclimate. Outlining trends in migratory and mobility studies, Holly R. Barcus and Stanley D. Brunn demonstrate that three primary factors are examined when studying the likelihood of mobility in an individual or in a community: economic opportunity, attachment to place, and community networks. In their interviews, completed at family reunions in eastern Kentucky, they explore more fully the attachment to place: "While out-migration is attributed to changing economic circumstances, and the restructuring of manufacturing and labor shortages in regions outside of Appalachia, return-migration is associated with individual characteristics, namely place attachment and family ties" (2009, 31–32).

Place attachment and family ties are strong features of the stereotypical cinematic immigrant, whether Latino or Appalachian. Barcus and Brunn, in their study of eastern Kentucky family-reunion attendees, found that a connection to place can remain equally strong among migratory Appalachians:

> In summary, these three categories of respondents shed light on the complex relationships between mobility, immobility, and place attachment. From these respondents it is clear that long-term residence in one location or community does not necessarily reflect a strong attachment to that place or even positive feelings about residing in this particular place. Rather, one's perceived social and familial standing or importance within the community and the quality of individual relationships seems to be a much more accurate gauge of place satisfaction. (2009, 44)

The perception of one's role within the community is arguably shaped internally and externally. Certainly, what actually happens within a community has a large impact on someone's feeling of belonging. External factors like images and stereotypes can contribute to one's sense of duty to belong, if not belonging itself. In both of the nondominant and migratory groups in question, urban Appalachians and Mexican Americans, perceptions of the culture-shock thesis combined with the outlier reputation can contribute to the trends that Barcus and Brunn reveal.

Cinematic representations of urban Appalachia create superficial empathy with the migrant but also reinforce stereotypes to show them as the other—perpetual outsiders in their new home. The inability to acculturate and the longing for home and links to another place mark the migrants. The narratives that depict mountain migrants tend to follow the patterns established to portray the Latino immigrant—and usually ends in tragedy. The only happy ending for these figures is a return home—to cease to be a migrant and to reify a national order.

▶ Appalachian Migration

As Phillip J. Obermiller begins his chapter in *High Mountains Rising: Appalachia in Time and Place*, he explains that his interest, for the duration of the chapter, is "not in migrants who became Appalachians, but in Appalachians who became migrants" (2011, 88). The same can be said of the focus of this chapter, taking one narrow category of Appalachia to understand a vein of experience and representation. Further, I narrow my focus to one phase or wave of immigration, resulting from the War on Poverty. While earlier migration had taken place, which often encouraged and facilitated the outmigration of the 1960s and 1970s, it was this latter wave that fully fleshed out and broadcast the type of the mountain migrant.[1]

Appalachian outmigration has occurred in phases, driven by economic turns as Appalachia was industrialized and entered a national market, now impacted by the turns in other sectors. Trends in Appalachian outmigration have, in some ways, mirrored larger national trends of rural to urban migration and southern to northern migration. Guided by industrial growth and economic depression, a pull toward cities and a push away from farms and mountains has facilitated peaks in migratory patterns. On a larger scale, migration to the urban North was influenced by sociopolitical opportunities as well. As early as 1910, peaking after World War II, African Americans sought opportunity, equality, and safety outside of the South. In Appalachia, though, the motivation to leave was primarily economic in first generations. Trailing migrators who followed family members or neighbors were also motivated by additional opportunities promised by the city.

Between 1900 and 1930 a 55 percent population growth in Appalachia led to a shortage of jobs, a shortage of land, and chronic poverty, as assessed by

New Deal investigators. The promise of work in the city, the active recruitment of companies, and economic shifts toward cash crops drew many away from the mountains and toward nearby cities. Outmigration did not happen all at once but followed a step migration pattern. The first step tended to be within Appalachia, as workers moved from family farms to coal camps. The second step was the shift to nearby urban areas like Lexington, Kentucky, or Knoxville, Tennessee, often followed by the third step of migration to more distant and often larger urban areas such as Chicago or Cincinnati.

The first of two primary peaks in outmigration in the first half of the twentieth century took place in the 1920s, as the timber boom went bust, anti-immigration bills banned European immigrants to open up the need for Appalachian laborers, and companies recruited mountain migrants to work in their factories. Carl Feather, in his analysis of Appalachian migrants to northeast Ohio, writes of this period in Appalachia: "In short, an area characterized by a subsistence economy had become moderately industrialized and partially integrated into the cash economy. The region had deindustrialized. The result was an area of poverty and limited opportunities" (1998, xvi). Following major recruitment of Appalachians by companies such as Goodyear Tire and Rubber of Akron, Buckeye Steel of Columbus, and Champion Paper of Hamilton, capable laborers left the mountains in large numbers during the 1920s. According to Susan Allyn Johnson, in "How the 'Rubber City' became the 'Capital of West Virginia': A Case Study of Early Appalachian Migration," many in this early wave of mountain migrants maintained close connections to home and worked only long enough to earn wages to return: "The experience of Henry Florence of Parkersburg, West Virginia, was typical. In 1911, he spotted an advertisement by Goodyear Tire and Rubber in the local paper stating that the company was holding interviews at a nearby hotel. Interested, he went to meet with one of the company's representatives who gave him a card that guaranteed him employment at Goodyear's Akron facility. After three years working as a tire-builder in Akron, one of the best-paying jobs in the rubber factories, Henry Florence had saved enough money to return home and buy a farm in Wood County, West Virginia" (2000, 111). Of course, not everyone who left the mountains for the city felt the desperate desire to return. A report cited in Stuart Hobbs's foreword to Carl Feather's book quotes a parent who praises "first-class city education" as a benefit of urban life. Single men liked it for different reasons. The same report includes a young man who claims, "You can live it up here. You can take a girl out on the town. . . . You can go bowling and you can go play pool and you can hear a good singer in a club and have a few drinks. It's not bad living in a city" (1998, xviii).

During the 1930s the Depression led to layoffs, which sent many Appalachian migrants back to the mountains. In Knox County, Kentucky, the returning migrants in the 1930s "increas(ed) the county's population by 30 percent" (Eller 2008, 11). Appalachian population, generally, increased 17.4 percent in the 1930s (Obermiller 2011, 93). In his 1937 study, *Migration and Economic Opportunity*, Carter Goodrich writes, "Many men who had cut themselves loose from the soil to take a wage job and were now cast off by industry were driven back into the mountains" (qtd. in Obermiller 2011, 93).

Through the Depression era and at the start of World War II, a second wave of outmigration occurred. Again workers were recruited from the mountains to the city for labor in booming industries. Statistics and accounts vary, but all agree that the peak years of outmigration occurred in the 1950s. Feather points out that "between 1940 and 1970, up to seven million people moved out of the mountains, about one million of them to Ohio" (1998, xiii). Kelvin M. Pollard's 2005 study, published by the Appalachian Regional Commission, shows that in the 1950s Appalachia's rural counties lost over a quarter of their population. This period witnessed a mass exodus from Appalachia to cities like "Detroit, Chicago, Columbus, Lexington, Indianapolis, Cincinnati, Atlanta, Baltimore, Washington, and Cleveland" facilitated, in part, by the huge coal bust that occurred because of a shift to electricity and mechanized mining that called for fewer miners (Obermiller 2011, 94–95). Because of mechanized and downsized mines, some miners returned to the mountains with the intention of farming, finding that the very work that had kept them adrift had, at times, damaged their lands as "industry had caused a great deal of damage to the Appalachian environment. Water pumped out of mines polluted streams and rivers. . . . Rainwater runoff from ridge tops denuded of trees washed away thousands of acres of soil, ruined creek bottoms, and even changed the course of streams" (Feather 1998, xv). As Ronald Eller points out in *Uneven Ground: Appalachia since 1945*, "When the boom times gave way to depression, much of the old Appalachia survived, but much had fundamentally changed." He continues, explaining that the natural resources, ranging from timber to copper, had been exported, leaving "Appalachia's human and natural resources . . . tapped to feed the needs of a modernizing nation" (2008, 10).

Cash crops had continued to make mountain subsistence farming nearly impossible. These difficulties, combined with a previous generation's ties to urban areas, made the move from the mountains inevitable for many. Like other migrations following World War II, a motivating factor was social. Eller explains, "This generation of mountain youth had grown up during the Depression and had been scattered across the globe by the war. They had experienced better housing, improved health care, and steady wages, and they had observed the comparative wealth of other parts of the country. Now they hoped for a brighter future for themselves and their children" (2008, 17).

Many mountaineers who left for work considered their labor temporary. Migrants from the mountains focused on areas closer to home, like Lexington and Cincinnati. In this period, though, ties to the mountains were tight. "The migrants, now more aware of the effects of boom-and-bust economic cycles, adopted shuttle migration as a survival strategy. Keeping their home places in the Appalachians, shuttle migrants became temporary laborers or, in more contemporary language, migrant workers" (Obermiller 2011, 90). Contemporary images of Appalachian migrants confirm this notion that "home" was elsewhere. A three-part story published in the *Chicago Tribune* in the fall of 1968 cites several locals who confirmed this sentiment. One man interviewed said, "If you stop any one of them on the street and ask them where they live, they never give you an address on Kenmore or Racine. They will always tell you Hazard, Kentucky, or Mingo County, West Virginia, just as if they were only visiting here and hadn't moved in at all" (Backes 1968, 432).[2]

In *The United States of Appalachia*, Jeff Biggers makes the claim that the region has had an enormous impact on American culture and history and has "endowed the nation with an enduring and conflicting treasure of innovations and innovators" (2006, xiv). Biggers asserts that "the great migration [during the 1940s–60s] from Appalachia might be the region's most important contribution to industrial America" (164). Biggers focuses here on the influence of labor unions moving from West Virginia into Detroit, but he is also making a more general claim based on the idea that even after mountaineers moved to the city, they retained their culture. As the saying goes, "You can take a person out of the mountains, but you can't take the mountains out of the person." As migration peaked and Appalachian communities formed in urban areas like Cincinnati and Detroit, a retention of music, folkways, and foodways influenced the experiences and identities of mountain migrants.

Like migrant groups before them, some migrants initially clustered in Appalachian enclaves such as "Chicago's Uptown, Cincinnati's Over-the-Rhine,

Dayton's East Side, Detroit's Cass Corridor, Cleveland's Near West Side, and Stringtown in Indianapolis or the Southside area in Columbus" (Obermiller 2011, 95). Urban Appalachians formed social groups, worshipped together, lived in communities with one another, listened to traditional music from home, and generally found ways to maintain ties in their new homes. Nola Hadley Torres's study of urban Appalachian women published in *Beyond Hill and Hollow* looks closely at second and third generations whose ancestry is Appalachian but who have either migrated to or been raised in Cincinnati. Hadley Torres found that her subjects tended to remain in the areas of Cincinnati where they had grown up or where previous generations had migrated. "Even with upward mobility and some movement into the suburbs," she writes, "many family members relocated near each other or continued to maintain close ties with their old neighborhoods" (2005, 51). For some the mountains were always home and the city was considered "the strangeness ahead of you" (xviii–xix). For many, including *The Dollmaker*'s Gertie, the consistent intention was a return to home. The daily task was to endure the city, save one's money, and make it back to Kentucky, or West Virginia, or wherever home was.

Their attachment to former place, adherence to tradition, and flocking together led others to see Appalachian migrants as outsiders unable to fit in to city life. University of Kentucky professor Morris Caldwell published a study in 1938, finding that Appalachian migrant families in Lexington "appear to be unable to make satisfactory social adjustments in an urban environment," a failure that respondents attributed to a lack in the Appalachian migrants, who were instead "adapted for a simple mountain existence" (qtd. in Obermiller 2011, 92). Studies like Caldwell's demonstrate and reify "the negative assumptions and stereotypes many migrants encountered upon leaving the region" (93).

During this wave of mountain migration to the northern cities, judgment and prejudice was immediate and evident. Resistance to mountain migrants is echoed in the language used to discuss Latino immigrants to the United States at the turn of the twenty-first century. A 1936 article refers to the resistance to the "army of occupation," and a fear of outsiders taking jobs from locals led to a 1918 ordinance meant to control "apparently idle young men with no ties to the community" (qtd. in S. Johnson 2000, 113). Appalachian migrants were referred to as snakes and invited vitriolic rage, as appears in this letter to the editor of the *Akron Beacon Journal*: "You and I know who these strike agitators are. I'll come out and tell you in the plainest words I know. They are these uneducated tobacco chewing geetar playing hillbilly illiterates from West Virginia, Kentucky, and Tennessee" (qtd. in S. Johnson 2000, 116).

These preconceptions affected the migrants in a wide variety of ways. Children were often held back in school, assuming that the mountain school system was not up to par with the urban ones. In the films *The Dollmaker* (1994; dir. Daniel Petrie), *Medium Cool* (1969; dir. Haskell Wexler), and *The Pride of Jesse Hallam* (1981; dir. Gary Nelson), the Appalachian children are judged by the teachers and perceived as underqualified for their new school system. In *The Pride of Jesse Hallam*, Jesse's son Ted is threatened with being sent back to junior high rather than retaining his place at the end of tenth grade. School administrators explain that his standardized test scores would keep him from tenth grade, but Ted's father makes it clear that he feels that the punishment is about the perception of the Muhlenberg County education and the school's desire to keep "briers" out of their schools. Transitioning from schools with low incentive for attendance or success, and without parental support and encouragement, many students became delinquents. This delinquency mirrors the culture of schooling back home but also reflects a lack of understanding and empowerment on the part of the Appalachian parents who "had little experience with bureaucracies and were reluctant to become involved in the schools" (Biggers 2006, 26). All these factors, combined with hostility or apathy from many teachers who "had difficulty understanding Appalachian dialects and knew little of mountain culture and heritage, except for popular stereotypes" (Eller 2008, 26), makes it easy to understand why the mountain migrants had higher dropout rates than their peers.

Another set of challenges faced by mountain migrants was securing a place to live. Although many migrants were drawn to cities and even neighborhoods because their family and neighbors from home had previously migrated, the establishment of a permanent address was a major obstacle to overcome. Over the previous decades some migrants were so unsettled and dissatisfied in the city that they stayed only long enough to earn enough money to return home. This pattern frustrated landlords and caused them to distrust mountain migrants. More generally, though, the stereotypes of the mountain migrants barred access to certain neighborhoods, particular jobs, and full integration into the city. Some landlords had policies of not renting to "hillbillies," and others who would rent to them "charged high rent for poor accommodations" (Biggers 2006, 24).

When Haskell Wexler began his research for *Medium Cool*, his "man in Chicago," Studs Terkel, directed Wexler to Appalachian "ghettos" to find potential actors and to better understand the communities he would be portraying. According to J. R. Jones in "The Lost Chicago of *Medium Cool*" (2013), Wexler and his crew, armed with coolers of soft drinks, pulled into the neighborhoods that Terkel had recommended. Wexler found that enclaves of Appalachian migrants were living in small apartments with high temperatures and even higher rent. Kids flocked to the crew and their coolers, and the filmmaker was able to recruit Harold Blankenship, a native West Virginian who played a young Appalachian boy in *Medium Cool*. The *New York Times* review by Vincent Canby describes Harold in an odd combination of terms—both flattering and cruel: "The most convincing performance in the film, however, is that of 13-year-old Harold Blankenship. . . . The child really is an Appalachian refugee and has the stunted look of generations of deprivation in his physique, in his eyes and in a profile that is as hard as a hickory nut."

The range of truths about the mountain migrants was not strong enough to counter the stereotypes about them. Stuart Hobbs writes, in his foreword to Carl E. Feather's *Mountain People in a Flat Land: A Popular History of Appalachian Migration to Northeast Ohio, 1940–1965*, "Most of the migrants were young men or young families with children. The average age of an adult migrant was the early twenties. The majority of migrants had an eighth-grade education; about a third had a high school diploma or higher. The Appalachian migrants tended to be from the better-off families in their community" (1998, xvii). Despite, or perhaps because of the challenges that they faced as newcomers to the city, most migrants adjusted and found success. A series of studies beginning in the mid-1960s and continuing still aim to measure the success of mountain migrants through a variety of markers. A study published by John D. Photiadis in 1974 measured "Occupational Adjustment of Appalachians in Cleveland" and found "more former mountain residents living in the suburbs than in the Appalachian ghetto" (qtd. in Biggers 2006, 27). The image of the welfare family with dirty hand-me-downs, homemade quilts, runny noses, and strange ways of speaking directly influenced the experiences of second- and third-generation mountain migrants and appeared clearly in films depicting the type. With a few exceptions this type has been solidified between 1969 and 1985, as the build up to and the repercussions of the War on Poverty have played out on the screen. The mountain migrant type is an important figure parallel in important ways to the Latino immigrant in film.

Mexican Migration

Similar to Appalachian outmigration, there have been trends in Mexican immigration to the United States in the twentieth century, most of which are demarked not by changes in behavior but by changes in laws. In the 1920s, as immigration was limited, Mexicans were "exempted from certain immigration restrictions and admitted as the first U.S. guest workers." Like other migrant groups, initial settlement led to continued immigration by family, friends, and neighbors so that a particular U.S. town might become populated with several immigrants from one Mexican town. Between 1942 and 1964, during the Bracero Program, 4.6 million temporary visas were issued to Mexican workers who were generally welcomed and invited into the United States. Immigration reform in 1964 and 1965, however, defined immigration anew, leading to an increase in illegal immigrants. In 1986, as the result of illegal immigration of the past two decades, Congress passed the Immigration Reform and Control Act of 1986. Despite this change in the status of immigration and the tone surrounding Mexican migrants, "the Mexican population in the United States doubled during each decade since 1970, with unauthorized migrants accounting for a majority of the growth, followed by legal family-based immigration" (Rosenblum et al. 1).

Since 1980 Mexicans have made up the largest immigrant group in the United States. In 1980 there were 2.2 million Mexican immigrants, and by 2013 that number had grown to 11.6 million. The sentiment that Mexican immigrants pose a threat to U.S. national security is relatively recent, solidified in President Ronald Reagan's 1985 speech, in which Reagan "asserted that the United States had 'lost control' of its borders to an 'invasion' of illegal migrants." According to Jorge Durand, Douglas S. Massey, and Emilio A. Parrado, this speech effectively "transformed undocumented immigration from a useful political issue (which it had always been) into a more fundamental question of national security" (1999, 521). The passage of the Immigration Reform and Control Act of 1986 marked the beginning of a fourth wave of Mexican migration. More than 7.5 million Mexican immigrants arrived between 1990 and 2010, according to a 2012 study by Campbell J. Gibson and Emily Lennon, which analyzes census reports and demonstrates this increase in population.

Appalachian migration was guided by a combination of economic pressures in and out of the mountains, cultural ties to home, and familial pods as a part of step migration. The same can be said of Mexican immigration, to some extent, though a more steady flow took place. Certainly, financial opportunities offered in the United States were the largest draw. The shifts, as mentioned earlier, are not in the people moving from one country to another but in one country's perception of the other country and of the nation's borders. Immigrants become illegal due, initially, to shifting laws. The passage of the Immigration Reform and Control Act offered amnesty to legally authorized workers but dissuaded businesses from hiring undocumented workers by charging fines and more thoroughly policing hiring practices. Immigration continues on an illegal level as ties to migrated family, economic pressures, and desperation push new immigrants across a secured and patrolled border, funded by the immigration reform act. Like Appalachian urbans, the Mexican American experience has been well researched and documented from a variety of angles. My interest here is in the newly formed communities of immigrants in the United States, which parallel the communities formed by urban Appalachians both in their establishment patterns and in their resistance to acculturation and their links to "home."

▶ Mexican Americans in Film

Familiar Mexican American tropes have been used to depict urban Appalachians as deserving of pity but ultimately outside of the norm. Both sets of films show the dangers of acculturation, establishing empathy with the migrant figures but ultimately showing them as best back where they came from. As Charles Ramírez Berg describes this category of film, "This familiar formula dramatizes the trade-offs involved when first- or second-generation immigrant protagonists (or sometimes class, race, or gender Others) set out to better themselves in the American system. In this formula, success is defined in upwardly mobile, professional, and socioeconomic terms and goes hand in hand with mainstream assimilation. (There is no success outside the dominant.)" (2002, 113). Immigrants are romanticized in film because they lose a central concept of self, are forced to disconnect from family and culture, and ultimately choose a return to or celebration of authentic self over assimilation—if the story is to have a happy ending.

The construction of these images told through these patterned stories makes evident the stakes of representation of the other as elevated and idealized but always outside. Ramírez Berg writes poignantly about these films that "want to say that cultural pluralism—diverse peoples bringing the best human traits to the melting pot—renews national ideals and makes America great" but instead iterate dominant and nondominant ideological differences. While the films superficially "celebrate ethnic Americans by showing that their traditions, practices, and core beliefs contribute to—and in fact are identical with—established American values," time after time in Latino and Appalachian narratives the outsider protagonist refuses assimilation. Instead, the Latino figure, according to Ramírez Berg has access to only the "sanctioned" American values such as "respect for truth and honesty, hard work, devotion to family, and loyalty to community (and, by extension, to the dominant ideology)" (2002, 115). The same is true of Appalachian access to dominant ideology. In similar ways, stereotypes have functioned to simultaneously romanticize and ostracize the immigrant.

The acknowledgment of these stereotypes, which is a basic purpose of Ramírez Berg's book and of this book, is only a step toward understanding. Linda Williams, in her article on Chicano images in film, suggests "a simple abhorrence of stereotype is not enough. The failure to understand the ideological needs served by stereotype leads to a contrary valorization of a supposedly realistic individualism that raises more problems than it solves" (1980, 14). Her sentiment is a guiding force behind my study, generally, and directs the analysis of migrant stereotypes.

According to Charles Ramírez Berg, these are the six basic stereotypes whose "core defining—and demeaning—characteristics have remained consistent for more than a century": "*el bandido*, the harlot, the male buffoon, the female clown, the Latin lover, and the dark lady" (2002, 66).[3] Like Donald Bogle, who analyzes black types in *Toms, Coons, Mulattoes, Mammies, and Bucks* (2001), Ramírez Berg discusses the cast of caricatures that have served as Latino images for the past century. The primary function, according to Ramírez Berg, is to sustain the superiority of the "great white hero" who is "the sun around which the film narrative revolves. . . . In order to prop the protagonist up, characters of cultural, ethnic, racial, or class backgrounds different from the hero's background are therefore generally assigned sundry minor roles: villains, sidekicks, temptresses, the 'other man.' Their main function is to provide opportunities for the protagonist to display his absolute moral, physical, and intellectual preeminence" (67). Whether the Latino/a figures are comic relief, sexual distraction, or villainous other, they continuously function as the outsider that draws a firm border to keep the white(r), more central figure on the inside. The alterity of the nonwhite figure, here as with African American caricatures, solidifies the dominance of the white figure.

Generally speaking, representations of Latino Americans have shifted across the century of their representation to both meet and shape American perceptions of this racial other. As Clara Rodriquez explains in her introduction to *Heroes, Lovers, and Others: The Story of Latinos in Hollywood*, "The history of film is a microcosmic history of twentieth-century America, reflecting some of our best and worst moments as a nation" (2004, xi). The phases of representation that Rodriquez outlines stretch from the "good neighbor" era (1930s–45) through the Cold War era (1945–60), the era of contestation (1961–80), and the postmodern era (1980–present). The height of the Latino immigrant or alien films was in the late 1960s and 1970s.

Films across many decades iterate the notion of the "alien" Latino who belongs "back where they came from" (Rodriquez 2004, 164). Rodriquez asserts that films such as *My Man and I* (1952; dir. William A. Wellman), *West Side Story* (1961; dir. Jerome Robbins and Robert Wise), and *Zoot Suit* (1981; dir. Luis Valdez) play on the idea that there is a natural order that has been disrupted by a crossing of boundaries—national and cultural. That Shakespeare's classic tale of star-crossed lovers from two warring families can be set in New York between Puerto Ricans and whites or that the comedic *Born in East L.A.* (1987; dir. Cheech Marin) plays on the presumption that anyone who is Latino has made his way to the United States illegally points to the larger issues surrounding a maintenance of dominant American whiteness.

As with African American and Native American stereotypes, images of Mexican Americans are no more carelessly constructed than they are accurately representative. In their article called "Teaching Mexican American Experiences through Film: Private Issues and Public Problems," Avelardo Valdez and Jeffrey A. Halley establish the power dynamic of stereotyping in films, reminding readers that the constructions are as much about the consumer of the image as the object of the image: "Films are discussed according to how 'reality' is not only constructed by those who experience it, but by those outsiders who attempt to represent that experience for their own reasons. In other words, there is a 'social construction' of reality and a cinematic construction of that construction" (1999, 289). These stereotypes are meant to reduce, narrow, set aside, and diminish the humanity of Latinos.

The particular character type that offers a clear model for Appalachian representation is the figure of the immigrant. Hardworking, family-centered, and religious, the immigrant type is characterized by a devotion to home, a longing for the motherland, and a deep desire to return. Younger generations are less likely to express this sentiment of connection to a former place, so the immigrant becomes primarily the generation of parents and grandparents. The immigrant who romanticizes the past is not always, but frequently, female. In his evaluation of social problem films, which focus on Latino figures, Ramírez Berg reminds us that the "obligatory happy ending metaphorically or actually sends the Chicano . . . back to the barrio where he began, leaving him to cope with the negligible opportunity that exists for him there" (2002, 112).

Hollywood films representing Mexican Americans and urban Appalachians rely on a similar turn that positions the nondominant as transitioning and othered. Frequently, the other serves to stabilize a white figure, but when the Mexican American or urban Appalachian is given the role of the protagonist, it becomes a story of loss and longing. He is necessarily displaced; a happy ending depends on a return "home" or assimilation.

▶ Mountain Migrants

Documentary films following and prompted by the War on Poverty heightened popular awareness of the urban Appalachian. As more and more mountaineers moved into cities like Chicago, Detroit, and Cincinnati, these experiences showed up on the silver screen. A spike in representations of urban Appalachians took place in the late 1970s and early 1980s, representing Appalachia and its outmigrants in varying lights but ultimately reifying the ideas that mountaineers needed to either acclimate to their new homes or move back to the mountains.

One of the most popular films of this movement was the made-for-television production of the 1954 Harriette Arnow novel, *The Dollmaker*, which aired in 1984. The film, starring Jane Fonda as Gertie Nevels, upholds the romantic view of Appalachia as home and affirms the notion that mountaineers belong in the mountains. In *The Dollmaker* the Nevels family finds themselves faced with the common and difficult choice of staying in the mountains with few opportunities or trying to make a go in a city factory. Clovis (Levon Helm), the patriarch, heads to Detroit first, leaving his wife, Gertie, at home with their children. During this time Gertie awaits word from him while she manages the farm in Kentucky. Trending mountain migration shapes the plot of the film as she, awaiting a letter, visits the post office and is surrounded by others in the same situation. Gertie finally receives word that Clovis has found work, so she packs up the family and heads to Detroit to join him.

Once there the Nevels family meets the challenges of the mountain migrant: homesickness, cultural dissonance, and discrimination.

Gertie and her children are immediately aware of their outsider status when they arrive in Detroit. As they arrive in the train station, the mise-en-scène situates them as outsiders. Gertie carries a handmade basket and wears an outdated and impractical hat, while the women passing are neatly dressed in suits with fashionable hats. As the family members step off the train, the children, dressed in overalls and looking mismatched, run chaotically past orderly and reserved men and women—many of whom are in uniform. As Gertie chases after her children, a woman says, "stupid hillbillies," setting the tone of the interactions that follow. Gertie is completely out of her element, but her children are more adept at navigating in the bustling station. Her oldest daughter, as if seeing her for the first time, says to Gertie, "You oughtta used your new purse, Ma," and her son chimes in, "You look like a body outta the funny papers." In these first moments in Detroit, the children assess their otherness by quickly processing the insiders around them. Ma's hat, her basket in place of a purse, her handknit shawl, and her general disarray mark them immediately as not only outsiders but migrant mountaineers. As they head to their new home in a cab, the cab driver says, "Detroit's a lot like Kentucky, eh?" The Nevels children are amazed and say, "How'd you know that's where we're from?" He responds, "I've met you at the station through two world wars. You're going back pretty soon." His answer situates the family in a context and in a migratory pattern and foreshadows the prejudice that will meet them during their time in Detroit.

Gertie and her family are immediately typed, from their first conversation with the cab driver to their interactions with neighbors. Gertie does have hope, though, that the schools will provide opportunities not available back home. She promises her daughter Cassie Marie that the library will be filled with books and that the school will be a welcoming institution. It takes little time for her to realize that the prejudice that she found on the street has also made its way into the school system. Here too the linkage between the foreign immigrants and the mountain migrants is made clear. As Gertie takes Cassie Marie to kindergarten, the teacher is trying to work with a Latino boy saying, "Garcia? Is that how you say it?" He speaks no English, and the other kids call him a "dummy." As Cassie Marie enters, Garcia chooses to speak to her, and these two outsiders are equated.

The school that the Nevels children begin attending services immigrants who speak many languages. Across the board, regardless of place or origin, the clear goal is assimilation. As Gertie talks with Mr. Spiros, the arts-and-crafts teacher who appreciates her whittling and basket weaving, he confirms that assimilation is key to success. In an attempt to reassure Gertie, he says, "Don't worry about the children. They'll be fine. They're young; they'll adjust." As Gertie asks him to explain, he says, "Oh, they'll learn to get along, be like the others." Gertie is not reassured but instead says, "I want them to be happy, but I don't know that I want them to . . . leastways not too much." Months later Gertie returns to the school to discuss her eldest son, Reuben. Gertie worries that he is unhappy and speaks to his teacher, Mrs. Stringer, about her concerns. Mrs. Stringer scoffs and says, "You hillb. . . you southern people who come up here. . . . Don't you realize that it will be a great change for your children? Well, Reuben has not accepted the change." Mrs. Stringer looks in the mirror, applying lipstick and readying herself to leave school, while telling Gertie that Reuben was prideful about owning a real gun. "I will not have lying and arrogance in my class," she says. Making clear the notion that a goal of education is assimilation, Mrs. Stringer concludes the conversation abruptly by saying, "Reuben is in Detroit now. He will have to adjust to his surroundings. That's the most important thing in life." Gertie gets the last word, though, as she reminds the teacher that "you can't roll out people like biscuit dough." Gertie is insistent that her children need not assimilate to succeed.

The harsh treatment happens even in their neighborhood, which is settled by poor people, many of whom are mountain migrants. A play-yard argument turns ugly quickly as kids yell, "Hillbilly! Hillbilly!" at the Nevels children. Before their parents break up the fight, one child yells, "The hillbillies come to Detroit, and Detroit went to hell!" "You're all alike. You come up here and for the first time in your life you get food in your bellies and shoes on your feet, and it goes to your head!" As the argument escalates and includes the parents, the father of the anti-hillbilly bully threatens Gertie by asserting his normative white position: "The cops listen to Joseph Daly. I'm a decent, respectable, religious American. . . . In Detroit, you gotta learn to speak English, you communist hillbilly."

Later in the film word arrives that Gertie's father has died. After the news of the inheritance of her family farm, she determines to find her way home. She trades their city car for an old farm truck, paying off the debt that they have accumulated in their time in Detroit with the money she earns as a woodworker. She has sustained the family by selling her whittled animals and children's dolls, which she carves out of wood. Gertie has worked her way out of a deep depression following the death of her daughter, Cassie Marie, by carving a huge block of cherry wood into the likeness of a mother and child. Although she is driven by a deep artistic vision, and is nearly finished with the block of cherry wood, she decides to destroy the sculpture, splitting it up to sell and to whittle. As she cuts into the sculpture with an ax, the low camera angle and nondiegetic music convey a sense of power and agency to Gertie. As she cuts into the sculpture, traditional mountain music returns, and Gertie seems to be working her way closer to Kentucky with every blow. Following this dramatic transitional scene, we see Gertie frantically carving small animals and trading them for cash. She arrives to pick up Clovis, who has been working away from home, and as they steer the truck south, all of the uncertainty, violence, and tragedy of the past year seems resolved.

The Pride of Jesse Hallam, a 1981 made-for-television film starring Johnny Cash, plays on the mountain migrant type in a way very similar to *The Dollmaker* but ultimately casts the city in a positive light, as a way to escape the poverty, illiteracy, and lack of opportunity in the mountains. Jesse Hallam is a newly widowed father of two from Muhlenberg County, Kentucky. Out of work and with a daughter in need of surgery to correct her scoliosis, Hallam sells his family farm for $15,000 cash, loads up the pickup truck, and heads to Cincinnati. The love of home and the ambivalence about leaving is evident in the opening scene, as Hallam stands over the grave of his wife, saying a final farewell. He is optimistic, though, as he pays cash for the surgery for his daughter, Jenny, and enrolls his son, Ted, in high school. Certain that he will find work, Jesse heads out—hoping that he can avoid working down in a hole, where he has spent most of his life as a miner in Kentucky. Instead, his own illiteracy, prejudice against "briars," and difficulty adjusting to city life make the transition to Cincinnati a difficult one.

Like Gertie in *The Dollmaker*, Jesse feels a deep responsibility to protect his children—who are struggling in different ways. And like Gertie, Jesse must humble himself to create a way to survive in a new world. While Gertie had to adapt to capitalism, cutting up her idealized sculpture into small trinkets for sale, Jesse has to—as the title suggests—swallow his pride to adapt to city life.

Throughout the film ties to Muhlenberg County are strong. Jesse, along with his children, Ted and Jenny, feel out of place in Cincinnati and recall the comforts of Kentucky. After her surgery to correct scoliosis, Jenny creates felt-board images of their farm and the mountains back home. Months after their arrival in Cincinnati, Ted confesses, "I been missing a lot of things back home, Daddy," to which Jesse responds, "It takes some getting used to, you know. New faces, new friends in a strange place." The strangeness of the place affects Ted and Jenny, but Jesse finds the good in his new situation and eventual comes to associate "home" with ignorance, poverty, and dead ends. In Cincinnati Jesse faces his illiteracy and works his way into an empowered position with a future that was seemingly unimaginable for him before.

The judgment of Appalachian migrants is present in the early part of the film, creating a sense of anxiety for Jesse, who is already ostracized by his illiteracy. When he enrolls Ted in school, the school principal and teachers assume that he will need to begin a grade behind because of the Muhlenberg County schools that he attended. They explain a set of standardized tests that will be given to assess his placement, but Jesse accuses them of prejudice, gaining the attention of the vice principal, who will later become his confidante and teacher. In the classroom, on the job market, and on the street, Jesse faces consistent discrimination because of his accent and the association that people make about his background. As Jesse seeks work and asks workers on a break about where to look, he is told to go back to his hollow. When he is stopped by a police officer, the officer calls him a "brier" and says, "You Kentucky briars come up here. . . . You don't know how to drive. You don't know anything." Jesse is haunted by the prejudice that follows him wherever he goes; his journey in the film is to overcome his pride and to meet head on the prejudice that keeps him from succeeding. Validating the judgments of others, Jesse learns to swallow his pride and embrace the values, structures, and lessons of the city that he is learning to call home.

Although the concept of Kentucky looms large for the family, there are no flashbacks and only a few romantic memories of the past. In the place of a romanticized Kentucky is the promise of a future in Cincinnati. The family who most influences Jesse, the Galucci family, convey strongly this idea of Cincinnati as a place for opportunity. Sal Galucci's status as an Italian immigrant validates his perspective. In one scene Sal says, "Back in my village in Italy, on a moonlight [sic] night . . . musica, wine, and soft women!" prompting Jesse to say, "You never saw a pretty, long, tall, slim mountain girl stompin her foot and . . . swinging that body around." They both appreciate the memories of the past, but it is Sal who directly appeals to Jesse, saying that if they return to Muhlenberg County, his children will be "nothing," like Jesse. Only in the city is there the chance to building something good, Sal explains. Jesse takes the message in and commits to learning to read, bringing his children along on a journey toward literacy and belonging. The final scene closes with Jesse and Ted side by side in a summer school remedial-reading course, and the last line we hear is Johnny Cash singing, "I'm just an old chunk of coal now, but I'm gonna be a diamond some day." The message is clear that acculturation, education, and assimilation are essential for success for this Appalachian family.

The 1986 television film *Smoky Mountain Christmas* offers a variation on urban Appalachian, reifying the romance of home and the cruelty of the city. The film is framed as a fairy tale, narrated by Dolly Parton, and begins with a description of a princess who lived in a castle high on the hill and is the envy of everyone around her. But, our narrator tells us, "When she looked down from her castle at the smoggy city of Hollywood, she knew that something was missing. She just couldn't put her finger on it. The one thing she did know was that lately she'd been listening to everybody. Everybody except herself." Lorna, a country-music star played by Parton, finds herself miserable, alone, and out of touch with her roots in east Tennessee. She is shown as a victim of a foolish and capital-driven music industry, complete with 1980s choreography and outrageous set design, which is misaligned with the simplicity of the song for which Lorna is filming a video. Fed up by being misunderstood, she returns home where she becomes a part of a strange fairy tale but ultimately affirms who she is . . . and what Hollywood had taken from her.

Stereotypes have their roots and formation in a particular moment or context. The stereotype of the mountain migrant, though it has precursors within other contexts, was born of the War on Poverty. The increased migration of Appalachian dwellers, combined with the heightened and propagated images of the mountains themselves, created empathy with the mountain migrants but also a desire to distance oneself from them. As outmigrants arrived in cities like Cincinnati or Chicago, their challenges went beyond seeking work, finding housing, and forming communities in a new social setting. These pressures were combined with active judgment, akin to the racism that affected Italian, eastern European, and Jewish immigrants in a previous wave of migration and that would affect Latino immigrants in following generations. The distrust of outsiders, the fear of job loss, and the need to assert oneself above another all contributed to the harsh welcome that many migrants met. This extended to Appalachian outmigrants, despite their status as Americans, the presumption that they were Christian, and their ability and desire to work diligently. Like the stereotypes of European or Latino American immigrants, these judgments need to be contextualized, as they say as much about the person doing the judging as the one being judged.

Mountain Migrant as Mexican Migrant

Herbert Biberman's 1954 *Salt of the Earth* and Haskell Wexler's 1969 *Medium Cool* lend themselves to comparison. Both films experimentally combine narrative with documentary film forms and techniques. Both are aligned with the political Left, exposing the tensions between the empowered and the powerless, whether the empowered is the mining company or the news media. Both male protagonists are entrenched in and a part of the propagation of the powerful, and both feel powerless. In form, especially, the films are similar, as they situate a narrative drama in the midst of conflict and allow the natural conflict to exist in the completed film. What links the films less obviously, but is of interest to the larger project of this book, is the similar experiences and representation of the central figures of the films—a Latino American and a mountain migrant. Both films make use of, and to some extent challenge, the stereotype of the cultural outsider. Both texts are situated in a history of films that relies on stereotypes of migrants longing for home, out of time and place, which allows viewers to romanticize the simpler ways of the migrant but also push them further from the normative middle space. These two experimental and left-leaning films rely on and experiment with the stereotypes that have shaped mainstream understandings of the migrant experience—whether Latino or Appalachian.

Films such as Gregory Nava's *My Family/Mi Familia* (1995), Paul Haggis's *Crash* (2004), and Robert Redford's *The Milagro Beanfield Wars* (1988) offer examples of the Latino migrant figure, while Daniel Petrie's *The Dollmaker* (1984), Gary Nelson's *The Pride of Jesse Hallam* (1981), and Henry Winkler's *Smoky Mountain Christmas* (1986) are traditional examples of the mountain migrant. I intentionally focus here on the experimental cinema verité–influenced films of two periods to begin to blur the lines between insider-outsider rights to speak as well as to complicate the notion that traditional Hollywood films rely on stereotype while independent films are more able to accurately capture the truth. As one of the interviewees in *Medium Cool* says to protagonist John Cassellis, "The tube is life."[4] Representation is at least as powerful, then, as truth. Whether in a low-brow made-for-television star vehicle, an independent film by red-listed filmmakers, or a film with a "political *X* rating," the Latino migrant and the mountain migrant experience similar plot turns and are based on similar stereotypes—namely an inability to assimilate and a continued link to home.[5] Both figures long for home—at times as a physical place to dream of returning and at times as an idea and a set of customs.

▶ The Latino "Migrant"

Salt of the Earth, narrated by Esperanza Guintero, opens with a description of a changing place that was once called San Marcos and was a part of Mexico. The family of Esperanza's husband, we are told, owned the land before the Anglos came and San Marcos, Mexico, became Zinc Town, New Mexico, in the United States. The Latino miners in Zinc Town are not all migrants, but many of them have come from Mexico to a seemingly welcoming town with a rich Latino community. What is unique for Ramón, Esperanza's husband, is that the United States immigrated to his family's land rather than his family immigrating to the United States. Nevertheless, the sentiment and the experiences are the same. The Latinos are offered lower wages, placed in more dangerous working conditions, and given lower standards of sanitation in their housing. The Latino workers band together, maintaining customs and speaking a mixture of Spanish and English (which could be primarily to accommodate an English-speaking audience). The traditional narrative of the Latino migrant centers on romanticized images of home. In the case of *Salt of the Earth*, there is no home to which they might return. Nevertheless, they are shamed, treated differently than the Anglo community members, and judged—ironically—as outsiders.

Similar but not equivalent to an actual longing to return home is the maintenance of customs. In one of the most moving scenes of *Salt of the Earth*, the community celebrates Esperanza's *mañanita*. Earlier in the evening of her birthday, Esperanza and Ramón have argued. She says that the men need to ask for better sanitation conditions in their demands of the company, while he quips, "You're a woman. You don't know what it's like out there. Leave it to the men," assuming that conditions refers only to mining protocol. He storms out, leaving a pregnant wife and two children at home. Their oldest son eventually goes to the local watering hole and reminds him of her birthday. The scene cuts to a sleeping Esperanza, awakened by singing outside her window. Traditionally, in Mexico, the community serenades people on their birthday at dawn. The voice-over narration explains the significance of this moment, while the warm smile that extends across Esperanza's face for the first time in the film makes clear how important this tradition is for her. It is as if she is not only smiling as she receives special attention on her birthday but transported to another place. The experience connects her to a different time and to the traditions that feel apart from the mines. The feeling lingers, as she reflects, "All the next week, I kept thinking of my *mañanita*. I had never had so nice a party. It was like a song running through my mind. A daydream to lighten the day's work. We all forgot our troubles at the *mañanita*."

Disregard and distrust from the dominant group also feature prominently in stereotypes of the immigrant. A contemporary example of a film that relies on accessible tropes is *Crash* (2004; dir. Paul Haggis). In *Crash* a racist and cold woman of prominence and wealth (Jean, played by Sandra Bullock) distrusts a Latino locksmith, solely on the grounds of his ethnicity, treating him as only a "Mexican," replaceable and without needs. After she frantically orders all the locks changed on her home following a carjacking experience in another part of town, she demands that all the locks be changed again the next day. When her husband questions this, with Daniel the locksmith in earshot, she refers to him as a "gang member" with "the shaved head, the pants around his ass, the prison tattoos" who will "sell our key to one of his gangbanger friends the moment he is out the door." In this moment Jean is threatened by anyone who is unlike her and lumps together not only all Latinos but all nonwhites, as she extends the blame of the carjacking by African Americans to a presumption about Daniel.

A similar disregard of Latinos (seen as immigrants despite their earlier claims to the land) helps drive the plot of *Salt of the Earth*, as the Latino community in Zinc Town begins to demand equality with the white miners. In an early scene of the film, we see Ramón lighting dynamite in the mine. An unplanned explosion puts him in danger and prompts a discussion among Latino miners about the fact that the Anglo miners are allowed to work in pairs for safety, but they are forced to work alone. When Ramón complains to the boss, he is told, "You work alone. If you can't handle the job, I'll find someone who can." Ramón responds, "Who, a scab?" drawing the response, "An American." In this short scene Ramón understands that his safety matters less than the profit of the company, that he is considered less crucial than an Anglo worker, that he is replaceable, and that he is not considered an American.

The plot thickens as the fight for equality between Anglos and Latinos crosses gender boundaries, which is a primary way that scholars have remembered the film over the years. As the women establish their voices and demand to be heard, the men begin to listen. While the men protest to demand safer working conditions, the women try to join them with signs that read, "We want sanitation, not discrimination." Eventually, women are allowed to join the protests, and their demands are included in the demands of the union protesters. Finally, the strikers are dependent on the women's participation in the protests.

During the strikes, which continue for the majority of the film and last several months, the mistreatment and lack of respect for the Latinos is made clear.[6] In one scene, as the company sends strikebreakers to assess the situation, a company man says, "They're like children in many ways. Sometimes you have to humor them. Sometimes you have to spank them. Sometimes you have to take their food away." Although the ending of the story is a happy one, with the strike accomplishing the requested changes—including the sanitation demands of the women—the disregard for and shunning of the Latino community by the miners persists.

Salt of the Earth closes optimistically: the Latino community is understood as perseverant, holding tight not only to their demands but also to their traditions. With very few exceptions the community remains Latino—separate from the never-seen Anglo workers with different work and housing conditions. The community has formed a close bond through their trials to fight the bosses, and their separation from the dominant community is ambivalent. Certainly, the film intends to celebrate the strikers and presents this as a victory.

The concept of home—as a place and as an idea—is a central marker of the immigrant stereotype. Used to evoke empathy, representations of home ultimately keep the immigrants on the outside. In *The Dollmaker*, the ties to home and the desire to return are poignant and ever-present and are resolved only when the hillbillies return to the hills. In *The Pride of Jesse Hallam*, too, there is a consistent desire to return home on the part of the children, but assimilation offers resolution as Jenny and Ted begin to think of Cincinnati as home.

In *Medium Cool*, as in *Salt of the Earth*, the concept of home is both geographic and conceptual. Eileen (Verna Bloom) and her son, Harold (Harold Blankenship), move to Chicago with his father, who leaves the family shortly after the relocation. This family does remember home fondly, in a series of soft-focused flashbacks, but they do not talk openly of returning. This sense of tragedy and abandonment haunts the family and creates the transience associated with so many Appalachian migrants. Harold's images of home are especially warm and positive, centered around time with his father.

The notion of the urban Appalachian as maintaining traditions and practices of the land left behind guides and influences representations of this character type. Certainly Gertie Nevels exemplifies this concept in a positive way that ultimately leads her back to Kentucky. Her whittling work, whether of small animals or wooden dolls, earns enough money for the family that they can return to their rightful place back in the mountains. Her craft draws ridicule, even from her husband, who is more eager to adapt to Detroit life, but connects her in a tangible way to her past in Kentucky, allowing her to return to run the family farm that she has inherited by the film's close. Jesse Hallam, too, uses his traditional upbringing to benefit him in the city. For Jesse, knowledge of farming and produce offers a transition into the city rather than a return home. It is his firm foundation in farming that gives him a sense of subjectivity and agency. He is hired and works in a partnership with Sal Galucci because he can identify a cider apple and knows how quickly lettuce will wilt. While Jesse uses his traditional knowledge to succeed in the city, and Gertie uses her traditional craftwork to return to the country, both are defined by their knowledge of cultural work associated with the rural life that they have escaped.

In *Medium Cool* Eileen and Harold are connected to their former life in West Virginia by a number of traditions. Her foodways are linked to the mountains, and his raising of messenger pigeons offers a reminder of his life back home. As we are introduced to the family, Harold is working with his pigeons on the roof of their broken-down apartment building. In one of the film's most overt messages, Harold is seen reading a book about homing pigeons, while Eileen serves a thin vegetable soup and looks out of her kitchen window—overflowing with potted plants. Harold's nondiegetic voice draws a parallel between homing pigeons and his family, linking them to a place: "The racing pigeon or a homing pigeon remains faithful to its mate, throughout its life, provided that the mate is present at all times. Especially when the male bird returns after a long flight. In addition, when a pair has young, this bond is even stronger. If, however, the couple is separated for an extended period, the male pigeon, not unlike his human counterpart, can be relied on to seek female companionship elsewhere." Harold's father has left the family alone in the city, away from home. Sympathy with the two migrants is built in this early scene.

Over the course of the film Eileen seems to be integrating more fully into Chicago, assimilating with ease. The narrative of the film, though, makes clear that true assimilation comes at a high cost. The more connected that

Eileen becomes to Chicago, especially through her new relationship to John, the more chaotic the world around her becomes. A strange scene at a psychedelic dance club positions the naturally beautiful Eileen almost as if she is costumed and playing a role. As she and John (Robert Forster) make their way through a strange evening, filled with experimental music, disorienting lighting, and confusing spatial arrangements, Eileen seems disengaged with her world, her family, and her former home. Just in case we might read this as a positive step toward assimilation, the evening ends with a moment of accidental and disruptive voyeurism, when Harold sees his mother kissing John. Shocked and hurt, Harold flees, marking the beginning of the tragic end of the film. Eileen's physical connection to Chicago, denoted with the observed kiss, fractures the tenuous connection that Harold held to Kentucky. Harold's absence then disrupts Eileen's attempts to connect in a new place.

The next several minutes involve long, violent, disturbing scenes of Eileen walking through the protests outside of the Democratic National Convention. Still dressed in her costume from the evening before, she wanders as if in a dream state, searching for Harold. The world around her is dangerous, and she moves passively through it. She gets swept up in a march, is passively blocked off in one protest, and has the general sense of dazed objectivity—as if the world around her is happening to her, rather than her acting within it. Her lack of agency marks her urban experience as negative and outside of the natural realm. As the scene closes and the film ends, Eileen and John experience a car accident, which kills her and leaves him in serious condition. The film closes without resolution, the Appalachian mother unable to find her son, the Appalachian son left an orphan in the city.

By the end of the film, we understand that they belong back in West Virginia. Harold's memories of his father seem to sustain and ground him as he wanders through the city, unattached and unprotected. The ambiguous ending of the film, regarding Harold, leaves a viewer uncertain how Harold will survive or whether he will feel the pull to West Virginia, like his homing pigeons. Wexler complicates the narrative that romanticizes Appalachia and builds sympathy for the migrants, but even in its formal experimentalism the film relies on established images of the mountain migrant, which draw from the even more established Latino tropes.

Chapter 4 ► Appalachia and Documentary

eature films produced in Hollywood have not served Appalachia well. Whether romanticizing or making monstrous the "strange and peculiar," the film industry has participated in setting the region apart, behind, and askew. The strong and often unconscious need to have an *other* has carved out a hollow in which a large and diverse region seems to fit—at least in the minds of the public. Throughout this book I have worked to show the various ways that films have portrayed Appalachian figures through the tropes long used to portray nondominant, nonwhite figures. Whether offering an idealized view of the virginal wilderness akin to Native American images or relying on the Appalachian figure as comic relief in the vein of African American stereotypes or showing the rightful place of urban Appalachians through the patterns of Latino American representation, Hollywood cinema has constructed Appalachia as the other. The power of these representations is evident on a logical level, but verification would require an analysis of reviews from a reader-response perspective that this book does not allow. For the purposes of this book, I hope that the parallel representation, grounded in Appalachian studies, has sufficed to prove the point that Hollywood cinema has misrepresented Appalachia. Questions remain, however, about alternatives to mainstream film. Outside of the narrative film, how has Appalachia been depicted, and what potential is there for Appalachia to be portrayed in a more complex way?

Documentary film seems an alternative with the potential to convey a more honest and complicated view of the region. While there are notable exceptions and opportunities to subvert a system that privileges the director, the stereotypes of Appalachia have made their way into even well-intentioned documentary films. The earliest documentary images of the region carved out a path that few filmmakers have been able to resist. Drawn to the staid images of poverty, family, landscape, and brutal living conditions, documentarians have consistently shown the same Appalachia.

As soon as historians, geologists, and botanists such as William Byrd II, James Watt Raine, and William Goodell Frost identified a place *as* Appalachia, the earliest documentaries of the region were created. As discussed in the introduction of this book, the boundaries of Appalachia were determined through gradual shifts in perception rather than actual disputes over boundaries. These perceptions were often formed by depictions, descriptions, and documentary evidence from the region.

In the eighteenth and nineteenth centuries, many writers from within and outside of the region collected stories, wrote histories, and published reflections about Appalachia. In 1728 William Byrd II established many of the stereotypes that remain today about the Appalachian region in *The History of the Dividing Line*, which chronicles his travels near the Virginia–North Carolina boundary in the 1720s and 1730s. He showed the "up-country" as primitive, lazy, and unkempt. Beginning in 1899 William Goodell Frost, president of Berea College in Kentucky, mythologized the pure race of the region as he wrote about "our contemporary ancestors" living in the mountains of Appalachia. He helped create the notion that the mountains were filled with people untouched by the passage of time. In 1924 Berea College professor James Watt Raine published *The Land of Saddle-Bags* as a reflection on the region that attempted to challenge the stereotypes surrounding drunkenness, violence, and laziness. He had his work cut out for him; these stereotypes were hard to challenge and easy to reproduce.

Many of the earliest feature films were set in the mountains, and, likewise, a few of the earliest documentaries focused on the region. Very early films, like *Sensational Logging* (1910) and *See America First* (1915), focus on showing the extractive industry in a lush, gorgeous landscape. These silent films primarily showed the beauty of the region and the "sensation" of industries stripping the region of such beauty. In 1931 a film focusing on Mary Breckinridge's Frontier Nursing Service was produced. *The Forgotten Frontier* (1931; dir. Marvin Breckinridge Patterson) included reenactments and was a celebration of services brought into the region, not unlike the first film celebrating goods being removed from the region. Even in these first films, the interactions between the land, the natives, and outsiders take center stage. With the exception of the panoramic views in *See America First* (1915), the documentaries began to establish Appalachians as people dependent on others for profit and health.

As Appalachia was portrayed simplistically by documentary filmmakers, a responsive tradition emerged, allowing those in the region to tell their own stories. In few regions is there such a catalyzing event that shifts the perception and future of a region as exists in Appalachia. The moment in 1964 when President Lyndon B. Johnson launched the War on Poverty from a Kentucky porch, media attention was focused on Appalachia in a pointed and focused way—intent on showing the world the poverty of Appalachia. In what George Brosi calls the "most dramatic rediscovery of the region," the 1960s was a period of both external attention and internal restructuring (2006, 203). Surveys of the period sought to situate the region, and to understand its ongoing challenges. Thomas R. Ford's *The Southern Appalachian Region: A Survey* (1962), Harry Caudill's 1963 *Night Comes to the Cumberlands: A Biography of a Depressed Area* (2001) and Jack Weller's *Yesterday's People: Life in Contemporary Appalachia* (1965) deal in various ways with the history and culture of the region. At times these texts seemed to confirm the newsreels taken by outside film crews seeking out the decrepit and impoverished, which drew and continue to draw criticism from scholars and inhabitants of the region. This focus on the region—both from a national political perspective and as a cultural and socioeconomic subject of study—led to the first real boom in documentary images of Appalachia.

▶ Documentaries from the War on Poverty

Images of mountain children both revealed a truth and shaped a reality, giving the American public a scapegoat, an other, a representation of the poverty that Kennedy and Johnson were fighting. These early images were captured by Associated Press photographers who visited the region and were reiterated for decades by others who—consciously or not—captured the same images again and again.

In 1964 photographer John Dominis was sent with *Life* magazine to document the poverty of Kentucky. His images, which reached a broad audience, convey a sense of despair, destitute poverty, and fragility. As James L. Werth Jr. (2014) makes evident in his examination of the War on Poverty from fifty years later, "President Lyndon B. Johnson reportedly declared the War on Poverty from Central Appalachia because he recognized both the hopelessness that had beset the region, where some counties had almost half of the residents below the poverty line, and the hope of what was possible if people were helped to overcome the crushing burden of economic hardship."

Johnson spoke from Kentucky to show the need for change and to politically affiliate himself as a savior to a people in need. News crews and photographers followed Johnson's path through Appalachia, seeking out the most impoverished areas and ignoring middle-class neighborhoods, urban areas, and any other images that challenged the monolithic scene of utter destitution. John Dominis and others like him captured, in undeniably beautiful, haunting, and poignant images, a face for the War on Poverty to present to the world. This face, and these images, set in place a type—an expectation—for future documentarians, photographers, journalists, and writers so that when visitors to the region sought familiar images, they made their way to the same rickety porches, the same coal mines, and the same family farms. It was in this way that Canadian filmmaker Hugh O'Connor ended up on the wrong side of a gun in the wrong hollow in Kentucky.

In 1967 a Canadian Broadcasting Corporation documentary crew led by Hugh O'Connor set out to make a film for Hemisfair, the World's Fair that was to be held in San Antonio in 1968. The theme for the fair was "The Confluence of Civilizations in the Americas." CBC producer Colin Low purported that the film crew headed to Jeremiah, Kentucky, because they wanted to "show the contrast between the lives of miners and the American dream" (qtd. in Cohen 2001, 293). Ardis Cameron places the crew within a movement of the time, writing, "Like many filmmakers who went to Kentucky, O'Connor's route into Appalachia was through the poverty pictures that migrated north during the 1960s" (2002, 416). As the crew finished up their day of shooting, they happened upon Mason Eldridge, black with coal dust, returning home from a shift in the mine. The crew asked Eldridge to sit in a rocking chair on his porch holding one of his children—before washing up, as was his custom when he returned home. Eldridge obliged, and O'Connor and his crew began capturing this rather staged moment, which seemed to meet their expectations and offered an image of contrast for their larger project.

According to David William Cohen, O'Connor had experience documenting around the world and "traveled to eastern Kentucky to record what they saw as 'appalling poverty'" (2001, 293). Perhaps it was O'Connor's experience that led him to feel comfortable taking these pictures, but as word spread across the hollow to the owner of the rental property, tides turned. Hobart Ison, who owned several small homes, including the one that Eldridge was renting, was told that a camera crew was "taking pictures of your houses and naked children" (qtd. in Cohen 2001, 293). Ison drove over, got out, and started shooting. O'Connor died at Ison's hands after asking him, "Why did you have to do that?" In his discussion of the shooting, critic and local Donovan Cain is still asking this question, which he "still cannot answer" (Price et al. 2000, 417).

The moment of Hugh O'Connor's death was preceded by decades of misrepresentation, intimidating cameras, and short-term visits with long-range effects. When Hobart Ison pulled the trigger, he ironically placed Jeremiah, Kentucky, in the public eye once again. To many locals he was a hero. To many across the country he was the face of the savage hillbilly. Ison's lawyer is quoted in the film as reporting that Ison had said, "I shot the man for what he was doing . . . setting up circumstances of ridicule."

How, then, can a documentarian record a situation that is complicated, a community that is impoverished, and a father who is blackened with coal dust and not set up circumstances of ridicule? This is the question that I ask in this concluding chapter, wondering whether documentary film offers a way to wrestle with a complex region without romanticizing it as a "peculiar land" that is better off flooded out and without criticizing it as a dangerous, lawless wilderness. Through the documentary lens, might the region find a new set of lenses through which to view itself and be viewed by others? Or will the documentary camera always feel more like a weapon than a tool?

▶ Appalshop

A strong regional movement formed in the late 1960s and 1970s, aiming to find ways to speak back to the voices and images that had come to characterize the region. Rather than letting Charles Kuralt and the CBS news crew speak for Appalachia, there was a push to find ways to define the region from within. In 1969 a grant from the National Endowment for the Humanities helped support the development of a project that, according to Appalshop's website, has as its mission "to enlist the power of education, media, theater, music, and other arts to: document, disseminate, and revitalize the lasting traditions and contemporary creativity of Appalachia; tell stories the commercial cultural industries don't tell, challenging stereotypes with Appalachian voices and visions; support communities' efforts to achieve justice and equity and solve their own problems in their own ways; celebrate cultural diversity as a positive social value; and participate in regional, national, and global dialogue toward these ends" ("Appalshop's Mission" 2016). The project was one of the five film entities funded by the federal Office of Economic Opportunity as a part of the War on Poverty—even as it was fighting against the images and documentaries catalyzed by the War on Poverty. As a result of the Appalachian Regional Development Act, Bill Richardson headed to Whitesburg, Kentucky, to set up the Community Film Workshop of Appalachia, "intended to train disadvantaged and/or minority persons in the production and use of film for the purpose of addressing the needs of their communities. Additionally, the workshop hoped to train its participants well enough for some of them to be able to find employment in the film industry" (Richardson, qtd. in Hanna 1998, 374). Appalshop, as it came to be known, growing out of the Film Workshop, was able to change the reality of the region, empowering locals through media education, but could also shift the perception of the region simply by telling various stories of the place. Diane Price and others describe Appalshop as the "famous Letcher County media 'workshop' that began in 1969 self-consciously to make its own home-grown images of Appalachia as an antidote to outsider image" (2000, 408). By 1970 Richardson had rented out a tire shop and had eight students fully employed there—creating the antidote to negative media portrayals, creating jobs within the community, and training locals to tell their own stories.

In his thorough history, "Three Decades of Appalshop Films: Representational Strategies and Regional Politics," Stephen P. Hanna offers an overview of the establishment of Appalshop and the trends within Appalshop documentaries over its first thirty years. Of its early days Hanna explains that Appalshop was motivated by a strong feeling that "authentic identity had to be constructed by 'insiders'" (1998, 378). Also influenced by Jean Rouch, one of the founders of cinema verité, Appalshop aimed to "let the subject tell its own story," as Catherine Herdman discussed in her 2013 dissertation titled "Appalshop Genesis: Appalachians Speaking for Themselves in the 1970s and 80s" (75). Herdman points out that the motto of Appalshop, "Appalachians Speaking for Themselves," aligns with Rouch and cinema verité. The surge of outsider documentaries in the late 1960s led to this need for insiders speaking for themselves and helped set up the divisive insider-outsider split. Filmmaker Hugh O'Conner's death in Jeremiah, Kentucky, stands as a symbol of this shift—a moment from which to measure documentary film about Appalachia.

The 1960s drew attention to Appalachia that ranged from destructive to productive. Kriss Heiks explains the period's influx of images: "Pictures of gray, worn shanties, barefoot children, and old cars left dead and abandoned on creek beds were ubiquitous on national TV sets in the '60s, depicting a people who appeared hopeless and helpless" (Price et al. 2000, 414). Although Allen W. Batteau is discussing a broader period and a wider range of writers, the ambivalence he expresses here provides a useful way of viewing what happened to and within the region in the 1960s:

> To the extent that Americans are richer for the recognition of the strange land and peculiar people that Fox, Frost, Kuralt, and Caudill have supplied we are in their debt. To the extent that billions of public and private dollars have been expended in efforts to help the people and develop the Southern Mountain Region, we are compelled to understand the relationship between its mythical images and historical realities. To the extent that Appalachian's construction relied on verbal figures, orchestrating metaphors and symbols into clear and compelling images—that is, to the extent that the making of Appalachia was a literary and a political invention rather than a geographical discovery—then to understand the Appalachia of American fiction, journalism, philanthropy, and public policy of the last century, we require today a poetic for Appalachia. (1990, 1)

The result of this myopic focus on Appalachia was positive in the creation of organizations such as Foxfire, Appalshop, and Appalachian Volunteers. The impact of these organizations is contentious—both reifying and challenging the stories and images about Appalachia.

Following the launching of the War on Poverty, with Appalachia as the "first battlefield in the War on Poverty" in 1964 and the airing of the CBS/Charles Kuralt documentary *Christmas in Appalachia* at the end of the same year, attention centered on the Appalachian region. Batteau explains the influx of donations and volunteers to the area in direct response to *Christmas in Appalachia*. As he puts it, "For several years afterward, poverty warriors, planners, bureaucrats, and the publics that supported them saw Appalachia through Kuralt-colored glasses" (1990, 7). The "publics that supported them" were not always met with open arms and gratitude, of course.

Following President Johnson's State of the Union address on January 8, 1964, the Council of the Southern Mountains organized to place educators in the region and expanded within a year to build an eight-week summer project in eastern Kentucky. Inspired by and modeled after Freedom Summer, Appalachian Volunteers was funded and then launched by Gibbs Kinderman, who had taken part in Freedom Summer in 1964 in Mississippi. In 1967 several former volunteers and those loosely associated with the organization were charged with sedition, after their homes were invaded and supposedly seditious reading materials were found.[1] The charges were eventually thrown out of court, but the image of Appalachian Volunteers as seditious was disruptive and eventually led to the demise of the organization. The Appalachian Volunteer experiment demonstrated the difficulty of bringing outsiders in to offer help. Antipathy to outsiders and a strong need for an internal counter voice provided context for the formation of both Appalshop and Foxfire.

In 1966 the Foxfire Fund was founded in Rabun County, Georgia. As Sara Day Hatton describes, "Foxfire's learner-centered, community-based educational approach is advocated through both a regional demonstration site grounded in the Southern Appalachian culture that gave rise to Foxfire, and a national program of teacher training and support that promotes a sense of place and appreciation of local people, community, and culture as essential educational tools" (2005, vi). The sentiment that catalyzed Foxfire—a desire to positively represent traditional culture—characterizes the first phase of films produced by Appalshop. Both Foxfire and Appalshop were reactive productions to overwhelmingly negative, albeit empathetic, portrayals of the region. Exemplary of this period of poverty portrayals with Appalachia as the backdrop is the 1964 CBS television documentary, *Christmas in Appalachia*.

▶ Post–War on Poverty Documentaries

The influx of documentarians to the region, the sustained poverty, and the solidity of the images of the region eventually led to resistance and a call for alternative documentaries. Pat Aufderheide (2007) links the establishment of Appalshop to the interest among documentarians in the region. The increased attention directed toward Appalachia during this era coincided with a shift in film technology, making feasible and portable the art of filmmaking. This interest in Appalachia, a renewed desire to represent the region in opposition to negative images, and an access to equipment launched Appalshop during a time that many felt that they must leave Kentucky just to survive.

Public-affairs films are the genre, according to Catherine Herdman (2013), that was a predominant teaching tool of the 1950s and 1960s. The civil rights movement, for example, was brought to the U.S. public in this genre of documentary. With a bird's-eye view of a situation, an empathetic tone, and interviews with "insiders," traditional public-affairs films present situations as problems that happened elsewhere. In its attempts to recover a voice for the region, *Christmas in Appalachia* fits into this authoritative genre that Appalshop was reacting to.[2] In his history of Appalshop, Hanna (1998) outlines the phases of filmmaking that began with films celebrating traditional folkways. Appalshop films tend to fit into the following categories, according to Herdman: public-affairs, ethnographic, and advocacy/activist films. One force that drove Appalshop, then, was a set of established genres with which an audience was familiar.

Another force may have been a more radical movement in documentary. When Appalshop began producing films, it coincided with the 1971 publication of "Guerrilla Television," a manifesto that aimed to decentralize television (Shamberg 1971). Michael Shamberg, one of the founders of the Raindance Foundation, linked the underground press with newly portable recording equipment to help create and encourage counterculture video collectives.[3] Deirdre Boyle explains that Shamberg's manifesto characterizes television as a "conditioning agent" rather than a "source of enlightenment" (1985, 229). While the early Appalshop films lack the hard edge of other "Guerrilla Television" productions, the influence of this radical acknowledgment that a camera does more than passively collect and that a newscaster might be invited to have a voice undergirds the very creation of Appalshop. Whereas Shamberg's "mediagenic and controversial group," TVTV, was overtly concerned with an impact on an audience (D'Agostino and Tafler 1995, 154), Appalshop seemed as focused on the impact on the communities producing the films.[4] Appalshop is repeatedly referred to in the language of mission or rehabilitative work. Looking at the early days after the Community Film Workshop of Appalachia became Appalshop in the early 1970s, Hanna states, "The grant proposals for this series state that the project was intended to correct decades of misrepresentations of mountain culture and history and that Appalshop was in a unique position to accomplish this task" (1998, 380). Appalshop was established as an effort to protect the community from outside representation *and* to create jobs to enable young people to remain in the region.

In the early days there was a belief that there was an authentic Appalachia to represent and that only insiders could accurately access and represent that truth (Hanna 1998, 381). The emphasis on "folk documentaries" was archival and "adhered to the mantra of 'letting mountain people speak for themselves'" (388). Short collections of folkways coincided with longer works such as *Buffalo Creek Flood: An Act of Man* and *Harlan County: USA*, which were more overtly political. Because of the focus on some of the early films such as anti–strip mining, some saw those involved with Appalshop as trouble-makers who were considered hippies and outsiders.

By the 1980s the insider-outsider dichotomy and the assumption that one's address granted the right to speak for a place began to be questioned. It became possible to collect and archive folk traditions, agitate against exploitative practices of outside companies, and speak against detrimental representations of the region—regardless of where one was raised. Further, that dichotomy that privileges insiders was challenged as a means of the same exclusion that had hamstrung locals for decades. Hanna explains, "As Appalshop itself has realized, however, mountain people must look simultaneously within and across the boundaries that define Appalachia as a region and an identity in order to promote non-exclusive regional politics. The insider/outsider dichotomy might lead audiences to conclude that Appalachia is an exclusively white rural space where people cling to traditions in their battles against externally controlled energy corporations" (1998, 410). The shift toward inclusion, the drive toward effective filmmaking, and the tie to education and outreach complicated in productive ways what might have become a monolithic organization set out to simply capture the strange and peculiar ways of the mountains from a closer vantage point.

It is in the midst of these shifts that I want to focus, looking carefully at Appalshop's Elizabeth Barret, as she created a self-reflective analysis of documentary, centered around the murder of Hugh O'Connor near her hometown in Kentucky. Barret (2000) admits that she can't remember how it felt when she learned about Ison's shooting of O'Connor. She was on homecoming court, was economically comfortable, and did not feel much of a connection with the people that she saw portrayed in the War on Poverty footage. At the same time, though, she didn't want the rest of the world to "think of us as Hillbillies," and she realized that was exactly what happened as news of the murder spread. Barret felt a sense of shame at this representation and a recognition that part of the blame went to a generation of filmmakers who had been iterating the same images of poverty for years. Barret explains her empathy with Ison: "While I didn't feel the same way he did, I could understand where his rage was coming from."

Barret lived in nearby Hazard, Kentucky, and began working at Appalshop when she graduated. As she began to see herself as a filmmaker, she wrestled with the way that the rest of the world saw her home state. She was keenly aware of the role of the documentarian in a place with such resistance to strangers with cameras that a murder had taken place. She took a job at

Appalshop and felt like she was "seeing a part of [her] own place for the first time" in the films that she saw made there. Barret explains, "These films were showing my place back to me in a way that was entirely different than the TV programs of CBS and Charles Kuralt. Those earlier programs served a purpose, but they weren't the whole story."

Barret's self-aware analysis of Appalachian documentaries and of the role of the filmmaker positions her and this film at the epicenter of a contentious debate. As Barret poses the question early in *Stranger with a Camera*, "Who does get to tell the community's story? . . . . What is the difference between how people see their own place and how others represent it?" What if, as with Appalachia of the 1960s, the stories are unbecoming? What rights do the subjects of these stories have to determine their position? These are the precise questions that guide Barret's film. And it is her attentive nature that enables her to hold multiple points of focus within one frame. Throughout the film Barret shifts from her perspective as a filmmaker and as a Kentuckian, but also includes both Hugh O'Connor's and Hobart Ison's points of view. Barret offers a model for Appalachian documentaries that neither attempts to absolve nor blame but allows multiple and contradictory viewpoints to linger. *Stranger with a Camera* offers the first model of a transformative documentary that can, I believe, bring productive attention to Appalachia without romanticizing or patronizing the region.

Stranger with a Camera opens with a collage of images of Appalachia, drawn from various sources and arranged in homage to Hugh O'Connor. He and his crew had developed a five-screen projection system, which is echoed aesthetically in the arrangement of images in the opening and closing scenes.[5] Ardis Cameron explains, "Juxtaposing images with image-makers allows Barret to keep the audience focused on the contested nature of camera work and the kinds of visual skirmishes it has historically produced" (2002, 415). Framed with these multiple images, which do not overlap or compete, the film follows this principle, as Barret moves fluidly among viewpoints. Rather than creating logical transitions from one story to another, as might be expected, Barret simply shifts.

Mirroring the framed images that do not fade in or out but are consistently and equally in view, the narrative circles back on itself without preference to just one perspective. We hear from O'Connor's colleague Colin Low that O'Connor "had instant rapport with all people" and that it was difficult to imagine him being "insensitive." We hear from Ison's family member that Ison traveled widely and was a generous neighbor. Of filmmakers more generally, we hear from locals who are appreciative of the attention given to the region and from those who were angered by the depictions. Resident Pat Gish says, "The TV people filmed what impressed them. And most of it was not the fine houses in the upper bottom. . . . It looked like everybody was poor. And the fact is that the majority were, but not everybody was." Her husband, who worked at the local paper, demonstrates the complexity of responses to the filmmakers who came into the area: "If you want to generalize, I would say that the merchants and the business people in the county seat towns felt threatened and the owners of the coal companies felt threatened, but the mass population, I don't think ever did feel threatened because all said and done, there was a general understanding that we had severe problems. If you're hungry, you know you're hungry." Both the openness among some residents to have their problems acknowledged and the overt anger that others expressed are legitimized in Barret's film.

Barret holds up complexity as a truth and refuses to try to simplify the narrative. What is different about Barret's approach to Appalachia? According to Ardis Cameron, "*Stranger* is an especially welcome alternative to documentary practices that tend to serve up 'ordinary people' as a way to signify the authenticity of 'this place' and generate topographies of strangeness" (2002, 419). Referencing Trinh T. Minh-ha's discussions of authenticity and strangeness, Cameron argues that Barret's approach complicates the sometimes passive reliance on insider authenticity and the ethnographic documentary's tendency to exoticize place. Rather than leaning on tried methods that simultaneously elevate and other the spokesperson from a region, the talking head with an accent, Barret continually points to this methodology. She pulls back the curtain, removing the fourth wall, and acknowledges the construct and power of the documentary film. As Cameron puts it, "It is Barret's ability to show us the ongoing complicity of camera work—its power to rob, to plunder, to produce, to shape, to reveal, and to distort, to inspire—that makes *Stranger* such an important and useful film" (420).

The tension of the power of the camera is the driving force of *Stranger with a Camera*. The tendency to see a filmmaker or a film itself as for or against, liberal or conservative, insider or outsider, offers too simple a way of understanding a messy and complex relationship. Diane Price praises Barret because she "wisely does not try to resolve this ambiguity. She carefully balances interviews between the two factions, the wounded and resentful insiders and the wounded and resentful outsiders. Even Barret's voice-over is one of calm neutrality. She allows the viewers to decide for themselves which, if any, side they are on" (2000, 411). Within the film itself Barret acknowledges these pulls as she reflects on her early recognition of the images of her eastern Kentucky home. Although the intentions of filmmakers and newscasters was generally good, the impact was complicated. Barret wonders aloud in her film, "Can filmmakers show poverty without shaming the people that they portray? I came to see that there was a complex relationship between social action and social embarrassment." This relationship has led filmmakers to lean hard on the prior to avoid the latter. Barret, though, avoids making a film that is overtly political and directly faces the causes that lead to social embarrassment. Her direct attention to these issues, when partnered with her allowance of ambiguity, creates a powerful film.

Scholars, locals, outsiders, critics, and general audiences have responded positively to *Stranger with a Camera*, praising it for its power *and* for its ambiguity. Laurie Lyda writes, "Even after watching the film twice, I can't place blame. I can see the perspective that explains Ison's actions, just as I can see a perspective that explains O'Connor's" (qtd. in Price et al. 2000, 413). Similarly, Herbert Cain explains, "To focus on Ison and O'Connor as insider/outsider is to miss the shape-shifting shadow of media imagery which hangs like a heavy cloud over the film. Somewhere in the middle is Elizabeth Barret, the filmmaker, struggling to find her own place in the events that occurred on that September day in 1967." Cain continues, "For me, as for Barret, there is no resolution, no peace, and maybe no easy answers" (qtd. in Price et al. 2000, 416–17). As a part of a roundtable discussion of *Stranger with a Camera*, Kriss Heiks criticizes Barret's indecision: "The implication that it is better to be silently exploited than to have the embarrassing conditions of exploitation exposed is nothing short of tragic. Barret's seeming inability to address this issue head-on creates a kind of wrenching and confused heartache" (414). Eventually, though, Heiks grants the power of the film, even if it is not as direct as may have been desirable: "Although the film provides no concise answer to the issues it raises, the questions are left to resound with a gut-wrenching clarity" (415).

Elizabeth Barret carved out a new space for documentary film when she created *Stranger with a Camera*. Her collection of archival footage, interviews, and first-person narration is nothing new. What is remarkable is her resistance to resolve a contentious moment in history when a stranger with a camera was shot and killed by a local whose fear of misrepresentation was so strong that he took the life of another. Barret set the scene for a new school of documentary, but, with few exceptions, the films of the next two decades followed the same patterns that had first set up the confrontation in Jeremiah, Kentucky, in 1967.

The two voices included in Elizabeth Barret's *Stranger with a Camera* juxtapose perspectives on documentary, reminding audiences of the power of the camera—whether to capture the truth or to frame one perspective. Anne Robertson Caudill, the widow of Harry M. Caudill, says, "The camera doesn't lie. It doesn't photograph something that isn't there." Colin Low, filmmaker and colleague of Hugh O'Connor, says of the camera: "It's invasive, it's exploitive, and it is not always true. It can be editorially manipulated." Caudill admits that "it is never the whole story," and we are left wondering if there is such a thing as the whole story, and, if so, how might it be shown?

▶ *Hollow* as an Interactive Documentary

Aware of, influenced by, and reacting against the history of documentary representation of West Virginia, Elaine McMillion Sheldon set about to create a new sort of documentary that would offer a new way of recording and presenting the region. Experimental and democratic in its production and consumption, *Hollow* (2013a) makes evident the intentional resistance necessary for even documentarians to resist the powerful pull of stereotypical images of Appalachia.

McMillion Sheldon was raised one county over from McDowell County, West Virginia. She frequently describes herself as the first person in her family to not make a living in the coal mines and recalls that her family encouraged her to leave home after graduation from West Virginia University, noting that she would be dissatisfied with writing for a local newspaper. McMillion Sheldon felt acutely and directly the lack of opportunities in West Virginia, "as she herself realized she couldn't return to her hometown and make a living in her chosen field" (Costa 2013). The tendency of young people to leave the area, sometimes called "youth exodus," and of the educated to not return, known as "brain drain," began to hold her attention. So she left. Eventually, she found herself in an MFA program at Emerson College in Boston, where she met many of the team members who would collaborate on *Hollow*. After creating other traditional documentaries, in and out of West Virginia, McMillion Sheldon decided to focus her attention on her home state.[6] In an interview with Shannon Carroll in the POV Documentary Blog (2013), McMillion Sheldon reflects on her decision to create *Hollow*: "When I graduated from my undergraduate degree from West Virginia University in 2009 and moved to DC, I saw most of my friends leave the state, and it was something that I had always planned on doing because there's not a huge amount of opportunity as a filmmaker. This is a story that needs to be told, it is ongoing, and young people continue to leave small towns across the country every day." In a *New York Times* op-doc piece, she frames the project in terms of guilt: "Today, I feel a sense of guilt that I left my home state behind to chase my dreams. I am part of the problem—the face of youth exodus—and I would like to find solutions that could help us return" (2013c).

McMillion Sheldon set an intention to create a film to help tell the story of McDowell County, the poorest county in West Virginia, with an average annual per capita of $13,345 in 2013. When she began this project, she did not intend to create an interactive documentary. Once committed, though, she knew that she wanted to avoid becoming what she and others refer to as "parachute" filmmakers, who drop in and leave again. She began a Kickstarter campaign and widely publicized the production process within McDowell County, which led to a more interactive process even before the format had been decided.

As McMillion Sheldon and her team formed, they knew that it would be important to set up and make known the goals of the project. This transparency is a key difference in their filmmaking strategy and the extractive style associated with the War on Poverty films. In *Stranger with a Camera* Barret says, "Others [filmmakers] mined the images the way the companies had mined the coal." To avoid such mining Barret and her team self-consciously set clear objectives. McMillion Sheldon, like Elizabeth Barret, knew that her community was not accurately represented in the nightly news. As she began collecting stories and filming in West Virginia, she knew that the issues of the region could not be easily resolved. Deeply rooted, complex histories of economic boom and bust associated with coal labor, along with the repercussions of loss of industry, could not be presented or solved in a traditional documentary. Rather than attempting to provide a solution, McMillion Sheldon sought new ways to show McDowell County as more than just a problem.

The choice to create an interactive documentary evolved over time. McMillion Sheldon explains in a conversation with Amanda Lin Costa (2013), "One of the advantages of creating a project like this versus a traditional documentary is it isn't a time capsule. Things can change." Costa continues, "She wanted to create something that would engage the McDowell County community and aid them in changing their future. It seemed a natural step to her, one that takes the idea of a social documentary and instead of reflecting a community, asks the community to participate." McMillion Sheldon loved the idea of not only a collaborative creation of a product but a product that itself continues to evolve. She told *Filmmaker* magazine, "We are encouraging a discussion and not simply accepting the fate of these towns. The idea that this is a story that changes over time, paired with the desire to create local change and include individual's voices in the process, makes *Hollow* a perfect project to push the boundaries for a multi-year interactive exhibit and experience" (2013b).

In retrospect, McMillion Sheldon explained to her audience at the DC Web Fest 2014 Summit the reasons she made *Hollow* in this format:

- ▶ An evolving story
- ▶ Community participation and empowerment
- ▶ User participation
- ▶ Develop online tools
- ▶ Exposure and global reach
- ▶ Inspire change through interaction

At the same summit McMillion Sheldon discussed her intent for the project: "Hollow will communicate the historical, cultural, social, and economic significance of southern West Virginia through user-generated content, interactive data, and interviews with longtime residents" (McMillion Sheldon 2014). These factors complicated the process of creating *Hollow*.

With only a few models of interactive documentaries, McMillion and her team had a daunting task to access a community, teach them to create documentary films, and be ready to edit hours of submitted footage. They also had to create platforms to hold and display the materials that they would eventually collect. The challenges were—and continue to be—real.

McMillion describes the project in *Filmmaker* as follows:

Hollow is an immersive HTML5 documentary that blends community-created video with footage shot by McMillion Sheldon. Thirty video portraits of McDowell county residents are distributed across five thematic sections tackling issues like health, community activism, and the influence of the coal industry. The project draws on dynamic data visualizations, but statistics are balanced with personal narratives to put a face on the numbers. To naturalize the project's interactivity, the design team made extensive use of a parallax scrolling technique that gives the story an uninterrupted flow. (2013b)

In her 2014 talk at the DC Web and Digital Media Festival, McMillion Sheldon discussed the issues with the "distribution" of *Hollow*, which costs $700 a month to merely keep up the server. When invited for a screening and discussion, McMillion Sheldon asks hosts to pay the server costs. The response is disbelief. Why should they pay for something that is available for free online? The ongoing resistance to and lack of understanding about the format of the interactive documentary creates real challenges around access.

When Elaine McMillion Sheldon visited McDowell County for the summer of 2012 to begin building the relationship with locals she knew would drive the project, there was resistance, but no more than she had anticipated. She knew well enough the history of filmmakers in the region, and although she had lived outside of the region for many years, she understood from her youth that it would be unwise to simply appear and expect participation. One wonders where such an appearance would actually be welcome, and the practices of anthropology and ethnography make evident the need—in any community and in any region—to establish rapport with the community one wishes to document. McMillion describes this to Alexandra Bradner: "Taking time to gain trust and truly getting to know residents before ever pulling out the camera was important to me. Parachute journalists and documentary crews have unfairly represented McDowell and I wanted to make sure the residents understood our goals, [and] motives and were on-board with the project. More importantly, I wanted the residents to take ownership of the project through their involvement with community storytelling workshops and video production" (2013, 231). McMillion spent three months in the area, hosting workshops to teach filmmaking and storytelling. There was hesitation, of course. Alec Berry (2013) shares Renee Boldon's initial concern: "She's used to McDowell County getting the short end of the stick and feared the documentary would further damage its reputation. Speaking with Elaine and hearing her ideas, however, changed her opinion, and she decided to get involved."

McMillion Sheldon's plan to engage with the community and give residents not only someone to trust but skills to take away with them seems to have worked. Josh Clevenger, a participant in the workshops and a contributor to *Hollow*, understands McMillion Sheldon's perspective and is resistant to the ways that McDowell County appears to the rest of America. He told Mark Lynn Ferguson at the *Revivalist*, "There's a drug problem in McDowell County. There's this problem and that problem and this problem. You can tell the world about all of our problems, but that's not going to solve any of them." He believes that stories are worth telling and that the future will be better, even if one documentary won't solve all the problems. Speaking of his home in McDowell County, he says, "It may not be what it was in its heyday, but it's going to be bigger than what it is now. It can only go up" (Ferguson 2013).

The community continues to be engaged in the *Hollow* project. McMillion Sheldon intentionally set up resources to continue to involve residents. The team set up a blog and granted access for participants to upload new footage as it is created. McMillion Sheldon told *Filmmaker*, "I think it's important for an interactive storyteller to give up a level of control and work with your team to discuss the number of ways a story should and could be told. . . . With non-linear storytelling you have to learn to come at your viewers with those impacts from many different directions because they are accessing all the content in a non-linear fashion" (2013b). There is not a moment when the production is a "wrap," and it takes consistent trust to allow the community to update the story—as if it were their own.

Despite the vast challenges, the crippling expenses, the initial resistance from the subject community, and the lack of models for the film, the response to *Hollow* has been overwhelmingly positive. In his review of *Hollow*, published in June 2013, Jason Linkins positions the film as an alternative to reality shows like *Buckwild*, which feature what he calls "rural poverty voyeurism." So unlike shows like *Buckwild* or films like *Appalachian Hollow*, this McDowell County *Hollow* is rich, diverse, and continuously evolving. McMillion Sheldon avoids easy fixes, complicates judgment, and offers tools to a county to demonstrate their own pride and enter a new generation with renewed hope.

Alec Berry (2013) offers the following praise: "*Hollow* isn't a solution, but it is a confidence boost, uplifting the county and reminding its people of their pride." Similarly, the anonymous review posted on IDFA DocLab (2013) points to the impact of the film on the community itself:

> Making limited but effective use of interactivity, this web documentary introduces us to 30 residents with a surprising faith in the future. . . . Elaine McMillion transformed the portraits into a multimedia collage containing an impressive wealth of material. There are video interviews, photographs, data visualizations, quotes and moody dramatic soundscapes. Scroll along and they pass before you like pictures on a roll of film. It is McMillion's morale booster for the people of McDowell, who are doing their utmost to keep hope alive.

Hollow was the 2013 winner of the Peabody Award, where it was praised for "combining imaginative story-telling techniques with web-only capabilities that allow visitors to experience life itself in both specific and universal terms" ("Winner 2013").

Both the aesthetic and technical aspects of the project have been celebrated, along with the impact on the community and the repositioning of McDowell County, West Virginia, in the consciousness of the American public. Jason Linkins offers lavish praise to *Hollow*, calling it "maybe the most magnificently presented, web-award journalism I've ever seen" (2013), but it is perhaps the praise from locals like Renee Boldon, who describe *Hollow* as "one way to put local people back in charge of their own stories," that matters more (A. Berry 2013). In the War on Poverty documentaries that Barret captures, there was a passivity among the people shown on those films that is absent in *Hollow*. Instead, there is active participation and contribution to showing what McDowell County is and what it might be. That participation seems to have no place, or a questionable place, in most early documentaries. The point is not that Elaine McMillion Sheldon is doing something new; the point is that she is doing something that more fully incorporates the subjects of her film. She has a deep understanding of the negative and stereotypical depictions of West Virginia and works to do more than simply react to them. With more patience, more trust, and more pride in the stories that she allows to emerge, McMillion Sheldon is taking away the power from the images that have haunted the region. It is in this way, I believe, that she offers a model of resistance to generations of images of an Appalachia as other. It is in this way that Appalachia ceases to be the monolithic other—the unwhite—as it simply and organically splinters into myriad images. Just as Elizabeth Barret intentionally positions contrasting perspectives on the death of Hugh O'Connor and refuses to resolve that tension, Elaine McMillion Sheldon invites stories that she cannot predict and allows them to exist side by side—like any other community's stories might. She does not attempt to redeem Appalachia. She does not feel bound to show only the good of the place. It is her deep trust and pride in the place that allows her to hold these images without a voice-over to tell us how to understand them. In fact, the trust is so deep that she does not even control the way that we perceive the images or the order in which we screen the thirty short films. In her laudatory review of *Hollow*, Bradner writes, "*Hollow* stops short of diagnosing, historicizing, or psychologizing the deeper reasons *why* we see differences among the residents musings" (2013, 235). We would not be surprised to find different perspectives in a generic American small town; why should we expect any different in Appalachia? This film, both in its experimental and democratic production method, but also in its empowering interactive form of consumption, is based on a trust so deep that it need not be named.

How is *Hollow* a model for changing the way that we see filmmaking? How does *Stranger with a Camera* enter the conversation about Appalachian documentary without neatly presenting a solution? Are documentaries resistant to the unconscious reliance on stereotypes and the reproduction of Appalachia as other? These questions have guided not only this chapter but my screening of dozens of Appalachian documentaries. If documentary filmmakers at least have the ability to resist caricature by showing actual people, shouldn't it be easier to create films that are more diverse, showing the rich and multiple realities of Appalachia? One might think so. I had hoped so. Instead, though, I have found that the powerful images that have been fed to us from Fox to Foxworthy have crept into self-perception, and the models of Appalachian documentary create a mold that is difficult to break.

In 2013 California photographer Stacy Kranitz published a series of photographs of Appalachia, causing quite a stir. Her artist statement read, in part,

> I did not want to make images that reinforced mass media's view of Appalachia as a poverty-ridden region. I also did not want to ignore the poverty and only showcase selectively positive things happening there, to offset these stereotypes. Both of these options are equally problematic. I do not make claims that I have any authoritative view of the region. Instead I want to carve out a new path that references the history of mass media's outsider, one-dimensional perspective while also immersing the viewer in a complicated history of representation. (2015)

Many respondents felt that she missed the mark. In response to Kranitz's photo essay, published on the *Oxford American* website, Ronni Lundy (2014) wrote "Appalachian Slumming." She takes great offense at Kranitz's participation in what she deems the "densely textured complex history that has been made even more complicated to unravel by the both witting and half-witted opportunism of cheap shots like this drive-by photo 'essay.'" Even worse than the "drive-by photo 'essay'" is Kranitz's role in the photographs, as she casts herself in roles as if unaware of the story she is telling. Lundy critiques "the even more grotesque than usual hillbilly-gothic image of the photographer herself playing the near-feral, barefoot, spread-legged mountain girl slut, one of the oldest and most demeaning caricatures foisted on the region, and women in general" and calls Kranitz's longer collection a "wet-dream of Appalachia."

While Lundy's response perhaps had more teeth than others whose jaws were left hanging, the sentiment was shared widely. It was with some surprise and a dose of hope, then, that I saw Stacy Kranitz included on the program at the annual Appalachian Studies Association Conference in Huntington, West Virginia, just two months after Lundy's response was published online. It took nerve to show up, and I thought I'd try to lower my raised cackles and see what she had to say. I wanted to believe that her insertion of herself into these images was intentionally evocative or some postmodern means of drawing critical attention to the images so long created by outsiders of the region. I knew that I didn't think that this had taken place, but I wanted to believe that she had tried. It would matter to know that she meant well.

The panel that she had meant to participate in had shifted to a one-woman show—a sort of defense, I anticipated. She was very nervous. She was vulnerable. And that brought out in this room packed with Appalachian scholars—the most nurturing and supportive scholars to be found anywhere—deep empathy. We wanted to help her through this. We wanted to show her why her images stung. As I sat in that room, I witnessed such a strange occurrence. The more that Kranitz talked—and she seemed to talk incessantly because she both did not know what to say and because she was terrified that if she stopped speaking, we might begin—the more that we found ourselves silenced. Yet our silence was out of kindness because there was nothing good that could be said in that moment. But something powerful happened in that space when a room of intelligent, empowered, educated scholars let themselves feel insulted. The cycle of misrepresentation chugged along. We were too polite, for fear of her obvious vulnerability. We held our tongues. She got the last word.

As soon as the session was over, we turned to one another with raised eyebrows. We met in the halls and expressed our rage, our shock, but also our sympathy for this poor girl who had been so confessional and so unaware during her presentation. So later I thought I would try to talk to Kranitz and explain why we were all so upset. I approached her in the lobby. We began to talk. I offered to try to contextualize for her why her photographs had been so criticized. And she looked at me with such puzzlement. Not well received? Criticized? But no one in the session questioned her. Everyone understood, she assumed. Our silence was our complacency. No critical analysis had taken place. No awareness of the detriment she was causing. She was at the Appalachian Studies Association Conference, and no one criticized her. She took this as our support. And I could not blame her. She failed to meet me for dinner as discussed. And I could not blame her.

It was during that conference that I began to think about the ways that these images of Appalachia extend further than my Massachusetts friends' joke about *Deliverance* or a student's image of a hillbilly. Those same images have infested me with self-loathing. They led me to New England for graduate school and encouraged me to learn a new way of speaking. They made their way into filmmakers' scripts, relying on easy images of nonwhites to avoid engagement with the unique position of the Appalachia figure. They guided documentarians down washed-out roads to seek the familiar images and to present the Appalachia that the world has come to expect.

Like Barret, I resist an easy conclusion. Like McMillion Sheldon, I am aware of my limitations and see myself as a part of the problem. Will framing Appalachia as unwhite be misconstrued as a lazy form of racism, seeming to insist that *we* have it just as bad as *them*? Will my alignment of Appalachian figures with recognizable nonwhite types reify the types that I mean to unsettle? How much, ultimately, can a book on representations of Appalachia shift the way that anyone sees Appalachia? I have asked these questions. I have wrestled with these fears. Ultimately, though, I conclude that I hope that this book can begin to draw critical attention to the ways that the region has been portrayed as outside of the norm. It is my hope that, by paralleling newly named types with more familiar tropes, the patterns of detrimental images will become more clear. I hope that viewers of films might think about why Appalachia is shown as impoverished in a falsely unified way, why Appalachian women are either sexualized as vixens or wiped bland as helpmates, why Appalachian men are shown as savages belonging to a former time. Whether conscious or not, these portrayals serve a purpose, keeping Appalachia apart from America. These films offer a scapegoat for America's neglect, poverty, obesity, greed, and environmental destruction. When we place that ugliness in Appalachia and show its people as unreal caricatures, falling into the same types again and again, Appalachia remains a place where it is hard to stay. Appalachia is shown—still—as the strange and peculiar place that is easy to forget. So mountains are blown up. Schools are underfunded. Counties like McDowell continue to die. And, most important, people of Appalachia begin to believe what is said about them.

In her poem "Boom Boom," West Virginia poet Crystal Good acknowledges the impact that outsiders have on a region. Paralleling West Virginia women with West Virginia mountains, and stripping with strip mining, Good paints a harsh image of self-hatred and desperation. When "them boys" talk about West Virginia women in a negative light, they take it because "any attention will do." The years of degradation catch up, though, and eventually, Good writes, the women "done lost all their dignity. They can't see no way out." The image of "them girls" as disposable, backward, and used up eventually becomes true. It is my hope that with awareness of these portrayals, with attention to what is at stake when Appalachia is denigrated, there can be enough resistance that the images do not become prophetic.

Appendix ▶ Appalachian Types in Cinema

The W. L. Eury Appalachian Collection at Appalachian State University is the type of place that can take your breath away. The depth and breadth of the collection can astonish. After researching Appalachian women online and in my own university library, I felt that I had covered my bases. In fact, I thought that maybe my next project would be on Appalachian women because of the apparent paucity of research in the field. Then I walked into the Appalachian Collection. I found the call number I sought and had to audibly chuckle when I realized that there were shelves and shelves of books that I had found nowhere else. This experience recurs each time I visit the Appalachian Collection. I find myself distracted by fields of study and collections of books that I had never imagined (Chitlin' Circuit, NASCAR, Doc Watson!). So when I turned the corner on the PN1995 section, where one typically finds books on film, I was prepared for shelves lined with the titles of Appalachia in film that Hollywood has been producing over the decades. I was eager to meet the company that this book might keep. Instead, I found only two titles (Williamson 1994, 1995a). Through excessive searching in the web of Amazon's suggested titles, I found one addition: Scott Von Doviak's *Hick Flicks: The Rise and Fall of Redneck Cinema*, whose subject veers into Appalachia on occasion.[1] I checked myself, looked again, and sighed deeply.

The silencing of a group tends to happen in rather invisible and coercive ways. Rather than overt critiques of Appalachia, there is "harmless" laughter. Rather than manipulation, there is caricature. As I stood in front of the otherwise rich resources that afternoon, seeing the slim offerings in Appalachian film, I not only was determined to add to that conversation but was confronted with the power of film to create and normalize a typology. In just over a century, Hollywood film has effectively marketed for public consumption and ridicule a region that is laughable and backward. And it is not for nothing that this has been done. The effect is real; the impact is powerful. People keep telling me that it's just a joke. But I don't find it funny.

▶ The Hillbilly

According to Ronald D. Eller, in *Uneven Ground: Appalachia since 1945*, those who disliked the changes happening in postwar Appalachia could romanticize the region as a "remnant of frontier life," and those who were in favor of progress "decried what they considered the isolation and backwardness of the place and sought to uplift the mountain people through education and industrialization" (2008, 1–2). The effect of both was an othering of the mountaineer. Whether Appalachia was romanticized or demonized for backward ways, the modernization following World War II contributed further to its image as premodern, backward, and old-fashioned. The types that Eller discusses in the second half of the twentieth century can be traced to earlier needs to normalize and regulate American identities.

In the mid-1850s, predating but perhaps setting up the local color movement that relied so thoroughly on generalized types to represent a remote region, George Washington Harris created Sut Lovingood—a model for many types that have differentiated since that time. Harris wrote, "Immoral, racist, depraved, and mean-spirited, yet utterly vital and free of nearly all constraints of social propriety and status, Sut [Lovingood] positively revels in his own animalism and crudeness" (qtd. in Harkins 2004, 19). Sut Lovingood was an influence on William Faulkner as he wrote about the Thomas Sutpen family and was a model for James Fenimore Cooper's Natty Bumppo from the *Leatherstocking Tales*.[2] What makes Sut such a central model as an early male Appalachian figure is his duality.

In "Where Did Hillbillies Come From?" Sandra Ballard argues that "As a 'nat'ral born durn'd fool,' Sut raises subversive and dangerous questions about human nature," unlike his descendant Snuffy Smith, who is closer to

the buffoon figure that no one is meant to respect (1999, 144). These two figures are born of the same genuine nature. Both Sut and Snuffy are laughable
because they are out of touch. Sut, though, is rooted in a deeper sense of morality, and the earliest iterations of Snuffy were more aligned with Sut.[3] The
hillbilly, then, is on the cusp of a valued purity and a disconnected naïveté
that has no place in the modern world. At this point of tension, the hillbilly
can serve as either the ideal native or the laughable buffoon.

The hillbilly, according to Jerry W. Williamson in *Hillbillyland: What the
Movies Did to the Mountains and What the Mountains Did to the Movies*,
is a broad category and does not always even belong to the mountains. Williamson is more interested in the role that the hillbilly plays to the American
sensibility: "It's the hilly sides of the American economy, the parts out of
the mainstream, that I'm interested in, and the conflicted urban memory of
necessary frontier rudeness that produces the rural fool who up-ends our
complacent assumptions about ourselves" (1995a, 16). Packed into this sentence is the heart of the hillbilly and the heart of the representation of Appalachia. At the times that America creeps toward industrial homogeneity,
a place like Appalachia arises to serve a role—to let America be America
again.

In his seminal work, *Hillbilly: A Cultural History of an American Icon*,
Anthony Harkins (2004) argues that it is the ambiguity of the hillbilly that
has allowed for its continued popularity and usage. The earliest iteration of
the hillbilly is oft-attributed to Berea College president William Frost's discussion of "our contemporary ancestors," in which he points to the tension
between past and present Appalachian dwellers in the 1930s. Harkins breaks
with tradition and begins in the early eighteenth century. Before Appalachia
was even known as a distinct region, forces were at play to create the figure
that would become the predecessor of the hillbilly. Harkins moves diligently
through these two centuries to understand the motivation for and the evo-
lution of the hillbilly figure. Situated in cultural theory, Harkin's argument
is grounded in the idea that race and class distinctions and hierarchies were
especially uncertain during several moments of these two centuries, and the
hillbilly figure offers a way of reading the establishment of whiteness and
white normativity. Harkins argues that postbellum images merged the hillbilly and mountaineer types as a result of local color writers. Taking this further, Matthew J. Ferrence, in *All-American Redneck: Variations on an Icon,
from James Fenimore Cooper to the Dixie Chicks*, argues that the "function"
of the redneck has shifted but "the limits of the Redneck individual [has]

remained clear: backward, dirty, lazy, sexually promiscuous, crass, more or less the Sut Lovingood of Harris" (2014, 16). This image conjured in the antebellum imagination offered a way of understanding an outsider endearing enough to pay attention to but ultimately comic enough to disregard with a laugh. A range of male Appalachian figures appearing in films across the twentieth century and into the twenty-first capture the limitation, the promise, and the threat of the region itself.

▶ The Heroic Highlander

One type, the most idealized and positive, is derived of the most positive traits of the hillbilly. He is the most legitimately heroic of the Appalachian figures, though he does represent this duality of character discussed by Williamson, Ballard, Harkins and Ferrence. In fact, the most heroic male figure in American culture, arguably, is Appalachian. Davy Crockett, king of the wild frontier, provides a useful beginning point to demonstrate the variance of types diverging from a common point. As Crockett is imagined and reimagined countlessly, the needs of both filmmakers and audiences are met. He is shown to have Herculean strength here but to be laughably naive there. In *Hillbillyland* Williamson carefully catalogs and analyzes the Davy Crockett figure, arguing that only years after his death was he transformed from a buffoon figure of ridicule into "a non-foolish American image of ideal masculinity," serving as a "useful symbol of male sacrifice for a right cause" (1995a, 82). Williamson analyzes several iterations of the Crockett figure as he morphed over the years in television and film reproductions. That Crockett offers a starting point for the divergent types reminds us that this is not about Crockett but rather about the needs of viewers and producers. Consistently, then, there have been needs to see Appalachian men as variously ignorant and capable, fearless and invoking fear, keepers of the land and disempowered miners, "pure stock" and inbred, masculine and feminine, godly and godless. The blank slate of the Appalachian man seems to have ties to wilderness and land use, family, and physicality. Whether the iteration is an overly sexualized mama's boy who knows how to stalk prey in the wild (think Jethro of *The Beverly Hillbillies*) or a gentle brute who defines himself as a father and hardworking farmer (think John Boy of *The Waltons*), the hillbilly reflects the shifting audience more than the shifting identities within the mountains. The persistence of characteristics leads to some general stereotypes. The most heroic figures are conflations of these types.

The Disney Davy Crockett of the 1950s aligns with, or perhaps spawned, a figure that I call the heroic highlander. There is a consistent presence not only of a Davy Crockett figure but of an übermasculine figure who is connected to place, knows how to work with his hands to shape that land that he loves, and is grounded by his family. He fulfills a particular set of American masculine values and embodies strength—of body and soul. And in the movies he is usually a hunk. The variety who chops wood and hunts bears might play the fiddle around a campfire, takes only the occasional swig of liquor, dotes on his daughters, and raises good sons. This mountain man is a gentle giant who should not be crossed. He has learned to harness his power but can unleash it when called on.

Jerry Williamson writes of this figure, "The alpha males in these movie offer clear lessons about virtue: they seem to be saying that to be worth anything to the race, which also means being good for women (though not necessarily for furniture), an American man might do well to be a hillbilly" (1995a, 153). The heroic highlander serves the purpose of illustrating the continuation of American masculinity as derived from the days of the Revolutionary War. The independence won by a connection to place and a desire for freedom appears again and again in the heroic highlander.

Songcatcher

In *Songcatcher* (2000; dir. Maggie Greenwald), Tom Bledsoe (Aidan Quinn) typifies the softer side of the heroic highlander. The plot centers on Dr. Lily Penleric (Janet McTeer), who visits Appalachia to record and transcribe traditional English ballads that have been preserved in the isolated mountains. Lily and Tom begin an affair, which forces her to see her misperceptions of savage mountaineers but also allows her to indulge in some fantasies around his ruggedness and strength, it seems. Bledsoe's figure is not imaginative but rather reifies the firm imaginings of the heroic highlander. In an otherwise reserved but positive *New York Times* review, Stephen Holden (2001) writes, "One character who doesn't rise above cliché is Viney's scruffy, hot-tempered grandson Tom Bledsoe, who after some initial skirmishes with Lily becomes romantically involved with her. Tom . . . is a romance-novel fantasy of the sensitive, soulful Prince Charming lurking beneath the shaggy surface of a rough-hewn mountain man." Holden's assessment fits perfectly within the tradition of the heroic highlander who helps viewers romanticize a land that—like Bledsoe—has a tenderness hidden past a rugged exterior.

Reviews of the 2012 John Hillcoat film, *Lawless*, continually respond to the figures as heroic hillbillies. Drawn from a narrative written by Matt Bondurant about the Prohibition-era drama of his grandfather and great uncles, the brothers of *Lawless* (Shia LaBeouf as Jack Bondurant, Tom Hardy as Forrest Bondurant, and Jason Clarke as Howard Bondurant) are clearly meant to be seen as the heroes. Lawless as they are, they are the good guys and the corrupt, effeminate, and disturbingly cruel law-enforcement officer (Guy Pearce as Charlie Rakes) is the bad guy. The trope of seeing criminals as heroes is hardly new, but many critics are not buying it. Frequent comparisons to mafia films situate the Italian American criminal family as central, with no room for the less mainstream, regionalized, hillbilly criminal families. In short, the Appalachian mafia is the other. Peter Travers (2012) writes in *Rolling Stone*, "*Lawless* is a solid outlaw adventure, but you can feel it straining for a greatness that stays out of reach. There's even a prologue and an epilogue, arty tropes signifying an attempt to make a *Godfather*-style epic out of these moonshine wars. Not happening." Perhaps Travers simply did not like the film, but the language used to characterize *Lawless* continually situates it on the margins, as a hillbilly movie. Richard Corliss (2012) writes that "it could be a diorama under glass at the Museum of Nasty People" and *New York Times* movie critic A. O. Scott (2012) writes, "This is weak and cloudy moonshine: it doesn't burn or intoxicate."

These heroic highlanders, like the good ole boys of the *Dukes of Hazzard*, are up against the corrupt revenuers and law-enforcement agents. As a family, they are endearing. They take in and nurture a disabled young boy, Cricket, and they defend the honor of a displaced (and beautiful) woman who finds her way to them. These brothers are ruthless and lawless but somehow we pull for them. We are pulling for overt masculinity when we do so; the alternative is the strange figure of Charlie Rakes, who not only is a corrupt outsider from Chicago but exists far from the realms of Franklin County's traditional masculinity. Rakes is perfumed, gloved, and coiffed throughout the film, and he is shown to have abnormal sexual tastes that serve to villainize him. Here, in an atypical twist, the mountain men are heroic while the whiter and more normative figure is the bad guy. Importantly, though, he is a northern city boy, which places him in a different category altogether.

The three Bondurant brothers fight back when agents want a cut of their profit from selling their moonshine to the mob. Instead of fighting to defend their illegal way of life, the family takes on the heroic position of fighting for the underdog. They avenge Cricket's murder, Maggie's rape, and the general greed of the urban lawmakers. Although it is uncertain at times, and bloody every step of the way, they win. They kill the bad guy and they survive. In an interesting postscript, we see the brothers several years later, happily gathered in soft lighting with their families—on the other side of lawlessness and as the clear heroes of the film. We learn that it is not a gun or a revenuer that takes out Forrest Bondurant but a simple accident that leads to pneumonia, marking him as not only heroic in an acute violent situation but memorialized nonetheless.

The heroic highlander has existed in various forms from the earliest days of Appalachian film. When Appalachia remained a frontier—not only of the imagination—America depended on this hero to hold American values. As that frontier shifted west and eventually closed, the American imagining of the highlander shifted, too. It became less ideal and more inexplicable, less heroic and more monstrous.

The Monstrous Mountaineer

The heroic highlander, when taken to one extreme, can take the form of the monstrous mountaineer. Whereas the highlander has a gentleman's polishing alongside his physical strength and intense knowledge of the land, the monstrous mountaineer is the man who has been left behind. Contemporary images of the heroic highlander show him having left his home (*Next of Kin* [1989; dir. John Irvin]) or having formed a tenuous relationship with the powers that be (*The River* [1984; dir. Mark Rydell]) so that he can survive and even thrive with his mountain-man status intact, if not always front and center. Contributing to the mythos of the highlander, though, is a struggle with the world around him. Even if he has made it, we must see how hard he has struggled to beat the company, survive the rugged farming conditions, endure the economic depression, or outsmart the Tennessee Valley Authority.

The monstrous mountaineer has not come out on top in these situations. Although his situation is rarely described, and ethos is left undeveloped, we often understand a backdrop of struggle and even trauma that has left this mountaineer in his monstrous form. He is savage and primitive in his isolation. He is disconnected from social constructs and norms, unable to contain his innate brutalism. In some instances the brutality has a sexual or otherwise perverse twist (*Wrong Turn* [2003; dir. Rob Schmidt]), *Deliverance*

[1972; dir. John Boorman], *Cape Fear* [1991; dir. Martin Scorsese]). An entire genre of horror films is devoted to the notion that just outside the borders of civilization there is a demented, savage, bloodthirsty man waiting to destroy outsiders who come too close. Emily Satterwhite's study *Hillbilly Horror* is devoted entirely to this phenomenon.[4] What strikes me as important about this category is the longevity of its existence. The horrific rural figure, exaggerated when placed in the mountains, has a history as long as horror films. Even before the standard horror film, though, the image of the dangerous mountain man has persisted.

In the earliest silent film set in the mountains, in fact, the Appalachian figure is one to fear. In *Moonshiner*, directed by Wallace McCutcheon for Biograph in 1904, the moonshiners not only run an illegal whiskey trade but fight back against the revenuers who come in search of the still. It is the moonshiner's wife, an early feist, who shoots a revenuer in the back. The treatment of Appalachia throughout the silent period focuses frequently on the moonshine industry, making evident the danger of roaming into the mountains. Although most films focus on the violence between moonshiners and revenuers or on interfamilial violence, the threat of violence is consistent. The fear of crossing a line and finding the wrong end of the gun is a trope that has been used since the earliest films, which Jerry Williamson makes evident in *Southern Mountaineers in Silent Films* (1994). The line between heroic highlander and monstrous mountaineer is fluid. Part of the strength of the mountain man is his potential to swing toward the monstrous, but he also has an ability to maintain composure . . . most of the time.

In *Killing Season* (2013; dir. Mark Steven Johnson), an Appalachian veteran of the Bosnian War is shown to have strength, savage prowess, and brutal instincts just beneath the surface. Benjamin Ford (Robert DeNiro) is characterized as a sort of fallen heroic highlander. Living alone in the mountains, out of touch with civilization except when he drives into town periodically for supplies, Ford has built a world around him that sustains him. An antique rifle on the mantle, good scotch at night, and Johnny Cash on the record player all craft a pleasant enough life. There is evidence, however, of a brutality and a sadness, which we first understand as a weakness, as he cannot maintain a relationship with his children. The years of repressed feelings, guilt about his war experiences, and isolation all work like a pressure cooker, and Ford eventually explodes into a skilled and cruel monstrous mountaineer. Emil Kovac (Travolta) tracks Ford to exact revenge for his part in the killing by U.S. troops of Kovac's family. Playing on the trope of revenge plots as well as innate animalism, *Killing Season* places Ford in the mountains and characterizes him as part of the landscape in the classic ways. In this masculine showdown, the monstrous is revealed, giving fullness to the otherwise quiet and reclusive heroic highlander.

Both the heroic highlander and the monstrous mountaineer share a set of revered traits. When used for different purposes, their knowledge of the land, physical strength, and connection to nature can become idealized or demonized, embodied by Davy Crockett or Max Cady. Both of these types serve variously to set the Appalachian figure apart, as outside of the norm. As Williamson explains in the forthcoming documentary on Hollywood stereotypes of Appalachia by Ashley York and Sally Rubin, "They are white people on the fringes of what the urban onlooker considers normative."

> ## The Lazy Hillbilly

Another stereotype that appears regularly in films depicting Appalachia is the lazy hillbilly. Although an umbrella term referring generally to a wide range of characters, *hillbilly* evokes an image of a listless, lazy bearded man in overalls who finds any excuse to shirk work and makes moonshine because it is the easiest way to make money from corn. This hillbilly figure is caricatured in signs and trinkets throughout the mountains of North Carolina, often shown sleeping, smoking a pipe, or both.[5] Never far from reach is a jug marked with the cartoonish series of *X*s, denoting—sometimes overtly—"corn likor." There is little of the heroic highlander in this hillbilly figure, but hints of the danger of the monstrous mountaineer. This snoozing hillbilly is likely to also have a shotgun close at hand. If not before, by 1972 and *Deliverance* the figure of buffoonish hillbilly was transformed into a threatening and dangerous, if ever absurd, figure. The moment that the unnamed men enter the scene in *Deliverance*, there is danger. This is made more poignant, perhaps, as it conflicts with the expectation that these mountain men are the descendants of Snuffy Smith, Pappy Yokum, and Jed Clampett. In a few words the tides turn, and the listless hillbilly is made monstrous.

The linkage between heroic highlander and lazy hillbilly is present in depictions of figures like Li'l Abner. His physique marks him as preternaturally masculine and powerful, but his naïveté grounds him in the realm of the comic. In moments Li'l Abner is shown as a Paul Bunyan of the mountains. As soon as he speaks or acts, though, any heroic promise is dashed. He, like the lazy hillbilly figure, is bound to the realm of the buffoon. Like his descendant, Jethro Bodine, Li'l Abner is unequipped to manage the world around him. For Jethro this realization is made evident as soon as he arrives with his family in Beverly Hills. He does not understand the modern conveniences or the privileges of the wealthy. We imagine that he might have been more suited back in the mountains, but it's unlikely. Jethro is most like the zipcoon caricature, who emerged during Reconstruction to demean a rising class of free blacks by demonstrating that they were unprepared for the responsibility granted to them. More generally, within the depiction of African Americans in the late nineteenth and early twentieth centuries, the coon figure was laughable in his simplicity. The lazy hillbilly, from Li'l Abner to Jethro Bodine and on to Larry the Cable Guy, exists for comic relief.

The rise of the comic hillbilly occurred, according to Anthony Harkins, in the late 1920s, after the failure of serious films treating southern mountaineers.[6] Films made following this decline of melodramas "helped to gradually redefine mountain life and culture as a site of comedic excess outside of socioeconomic reality rather than a serious social problem" (2004, 152). Buster Keaton's 1923 *Our Hospitality* played on the Hatfield-McCoy feud, framed as a silent comedy. Other similar films followed, though the most notable for its inspiration of the comedic hillbilly was the 1938 *Kentucky Moonshine* (dir. Darryl Zanuck). The script notes a "typical lazy hillbilly scene," yet the influence of cartoonists like Al Capp, cartoonist known for his Li'l Abner strip, shifts the caricatures fully to the comedic. These early images of comedic hillbillies remained relatively unchanged for decades to come.

▶ The Drudge

As the region was constructed in the nineteenth century, the mountain woman, too, was imagined. The mountain woman of developing yore was hardworking—equal almost to the strength of the men around her. She was bound to her land, which was frequently shown to be nearly uninhabitable and difficult to farm. She was fertile but not warmly maternal. And she was uncertain of outsiders. These characteristics of mountain women form one of the longest lasting stereotypes: the drudge.

In 1903, in an article for *Harper's New Monthly Magazine*, Julian Ralph wrote of Appalachian women: "What I have seen of the girls and whatever I have heard of them and their mothers has roused my pity. The oldest daughter of these almost always large mountain families is almost certain to begin her life of drudging while very young, and as the women are all drudges after marriage and are married in childhood, drudging is their lot until they die" (41). The Appalachian drudge—a woman passively and silently accepting her backbreaking lot—was solidified as a type by the turn of the century. Lacking a careful ethnographer's perception and acknowledgment of subject-object relations, outsider's brief encounters or mere observations misrepresented or at least simplified mountain women. A quiet woman laboring alongside her husband was perceived as a drudge, worthy of "pity." Like the mammy figure, conceived a century earlier by outsiders who rarely took the time to talk to the women they represented, the drudge was assumed to put her own needs aside to serve as a helpmate.

In moments the depictions of the drudge were meant to rouse sympathy and even action in support of the region. In a 1924 study commissioned by the Council of Women for Home Missions and the Missionary Education Movement of the United States and Canada titled *The Land of Saddle-Bags: A Study of the Mountain People of Appalachia*, author James Watt Raine characterizes the Appalachian woman as follows: "She works a sixteen-hour day, scarcely gets one baby weaned before another arrives, and for wages gets a home, the blessings of copious motherhood, and the privilege of wearing her husband's name on her tombstone, which, with all her endurance is sometimes settled upon her before she is fifty" (1924, 91). For Raine, and for the councils employing him, the outside world needs to see mountain women as imprisoned by their circumstances. His depiction, therefore, offers a rather monolithic image of women who need the salvation of the missionary movement. The women that James Watt Raine and Julian Ralph observe remain silent, while outsider male voices speak for them. Importantly, though, these outsider male voices reflect and construct a "truth" about the laboring woman of the mountains, which has made its way into literature and film depicting the region.

As the twentieth century unfolded, outsiders wrote alternatingly romanticizing and horrifying descriptions of Appalachian women, all of which infantilized and silenced them. In 1933, in *Hollow Folk*, Mandel Sherman and Thomas E. Henry describe an observation of mountain women as they listen with rapt attention to the story of Goldilocks and the three bears: "But these are not wide-eyed three-year-olds. They are the mothers of large families. They have tramped in, barefoot, from their isolated cabins over mountain pathways and the dried courses of brooks to hear once more about Goldilocks." Sherman and Henry do not stop there, but go further to make clear their understanding of these women whom they are observing. They continue by writing, "for in some respects they are children with the interests of children" (111). To treat mothers and wives and members of a community as children is to take away power, voice, and range of experiences; it is a lazy way of depicting a way of life, and it works to disempower the object of the gaze.

The construction of a hardworking, silent woman who can produce so many children but still is herself a child prevailed in the journalistic observations of women in the region. This had become a stock image by the 1930s, leading Muriel Earley Sheppard to defend against this typing in *Cabins in the Laurel*:

> The mountain women are not at all the inarticulate, beaten-down drudges an outlander fancies them to be. He is apt to mistake reserve for inability at expression and poised composure for lethargy. There is nothing drab about a mountain woman when she knows you. The casual traveller, seeing a spare, tanned woman in old clothes, bending over a hoe in a cornfield so steep that she might fall the length of it, assumes that she is put upon, without considering what she herself thinks about it. (1991, 180–81)

Harry Caudill's *Night Comes to the Cumberlands* (2001) has been called the "master narrative" of Appalachia, inviting controversy, defense, support, and the attention of the American public at large. He glossed over the experiences of women specifically but painted a picture of the 1950s and 1960s in Appalachia that is a continuation of Sheppard's analysis of "beaten-down drudges" (Tucker 2003, 114). Caudill refers to mountaineers as "embittered rejects and outcasts from the shores of Europe—as cynical, hardened and bitter a lot as can be imagined outside prison walls": silently toiling, wildly impoverished, distinctly uncultured (2001, 13). Caudill's image of Appalachia, which would be framed by filmmakers over at least the next two decades, merely extends the image of the mountain drudge.

Caudill drew focus on a world from which the rest of America wanted to look away. The resulting influx of journalists, news reporters, and documentarians only tightened that focus, making more evident the perceived differences between "us" and "them." The result of this period of active negative representation, regardless of the intention, is difficult to overstate. Between the mid-1960s and 1971, organizing efforts to help support Appalachia were built and eventually splintered. The history of the period has been well documented elsewhere, but a brief overview as pertains to the representation of the region is worthwhile. In brief, the Office of Economic Opportunity was established in 1964 to administer the War on Poverty initiatives but had the "dual effect of reviving national interest in Appalachia and sparking a new debate over the scholarly treatment of its history and culture," according to John Glen in "The War on Poverty in Appalachia: A Preliminary Report," published in 1989. The Office of Economic Opportunity, Appalachian Volunteers, Council of the Southern Mountains, and Volunteers in Service to America are among the players who ushered in movements that both helped establish and support antipoverty initiatives in the region. By 1966, though, a significant splintering had occurred, resulting in the new placement of Loyal Jones as director of the Council of the Southern Mountains and the eventual end to the Appalachian Volunteers program. By 1971 the Council of the Southern Mountains, which had been established in and active since 1913, had disbanded over internal disputes and a lack of consensus about, essentially, how important a consensus might be for such an organization. As organizers and policy makers wrestled with issues of organization, a region was being shown as impoverished because they were resistant to change. Much of this representation is the result of negative responses due to organizational infighting. When individual organizers disagreed and failed to make "progress," it was easy to blame the people they had purported to assist. According to Earl Redwine, with the Council of the Southern Mountains, the program had become "the Christmas basket-for-the-poor charity worker's paradise," which only strengthened negative perceptions that Appalachian people were poor because they were lazy (qtd. in Glen 1989, 45). A movement that intended to help poor people of Appalachia escape the systemic oppression that kept them a world apart from the remainder of America, it was said, served only to create new sets of stereotypes and confirm long-held beliefs about the mountaineers.

While these representations were not specific to women of the region, the image of the Appalachian drudge was most vivid in these depictions. A closer look, however, makes evident the presence and strength of a second female type—the feist. Interestingly, the same women can be perceived as drudges from one perspective when another, closer look reveals a strength that would later become threatening. A figure like Ella Garth in the 1960 film *Wild River* offers an example.

Wild River

Elia Kazin's 1960 film treats the tension between the Tennessee Valley Authority and landowners, whose claims to property conflict with the authority's plans to harness rivers to create power. The opening scene includes footage of flooding that became all too familiar to those living on or around the Tennessee River and its estuaries. Ella Garth (Jo Van Fleet) is a matriarch who refuses to sell her land to the government and who establishes herself on the border of drudge and feist. To an outsider like Chuck Glover (Montgomery Clift), who arrives to force Garth off her land, she seems to be backward and old-fashioned. Ella says of the proposed hydroelectric dam, "I like things running wild, like nature made it." She seems of the past, but, as A. H. Weiler's 1960 *New York Times* review makes clear, she "is not merely a cantankerous old fuddy-duddy." In fact, she is racially progressive and forward-thinking in terms of gender. She is more independent and fierce, even, than her widowed (and beautiful) granddaughter Carol (Lee Remick) who inevitably falls in love with the Tennessee Valley Authority man from up north.

In moments Ella appears to fit the role of the drudge, as she makes clear her choice to forgo developments that would, in fact, make her life easier. With power, she is told, her life would be better. She understands this, though, and emerges as more feist than drudge, though to outsiders who fail to take the time to talk with and fully understand her, Ella is like the women of the Raine narratives of yore, drudging along.

Mae Garvey in the 1984 film *The River* offers another example. On the heels of the collapse of the Appalachian Volunteers and the Council of the Southern Mountains, Kathy Kahn published *Hillbilly Women* in 1972. Her collection challenged the careful reader but reiterated for the casual observer the stereotypes established during the previous centuries and reified after the War on Poverty. The nineteen women's narratives in this collection are disparate in their experiences but united by their focus on labor unions and activism. They are also united by their sense of pride. Kahn explains this tension, which is central to her *Hillbilly Women*: "The women in this book . . . have a pride in their heritage and their traditions. They have all spent most of their lives laboring under brutal living and working conditions. And, while they are proud, they are also angry with a country that makes their life a nightmare" (4).

Kahn's collection reveals the depths of intersection between the perceived drudge and feist. Her work—and the need for her work—makes evident the establishment of the drudge figure:

> Being a miner's wife means much more than the everyday drudgery of household chores and raising babies. It means struggling every day to eliminate coal dust from furniture, bed clothes, table tops, and children's bodies. It means being your

own doctor, because there isn't a clinic nearby and there is no money to pay for one anyway. It means giving children the only education they will ever get outside of a few inadequate lessons in poorly run schoolhouses. It means, most of all, waiting. (1972, xviii–xix)

As Kahn introduces the Appalachian women of her collection, she frames them in the expectations of the reader. She acknowledges the images that most will bring to the narratives. She does so even more explicitly when she explains that the women who have fought in vain with coal companies "are the women who are usually pictured in articles and books as mournful creatures, covered with dust and grime, their thin mouths hardened into a grim expression. Typically, the women are seen as hopeless, helpless, and passive" (xx). These images of drudgery, passivity, and mournfulness were well established again and again over the past century, and while they are complicated in a book like Kahn's, they still offer a solid grounding on which a reader might stand to read about these "Hillbilly Women."

Images of drudges in Appalachia prevailed well into the 1970s as the War on Poverty–inspired documentarians and journalists visited regions long enough to photograph the shocking and interview the stunning. In documentary and journalistic footage, the Appalachian drudge was central to the broad generalization of the region and provided an effective method to evoke empathy while maintaining distance. The same is true for many fictional films set in Appalachia. Directors relied on silent, hardworking, aged, and sexless women as a part of the mise-en-scène more than the cast. Though not entirely fictional, this stereotype evoked pity from outsiders by othering the insider.

Sargent York

The drudging mother is a frequent feature of Appalachian film, working to create a connection to the Appalachian woman, though it is generally through the relationship of the (usually) male protagonist. *Sargent York* provides an early model for this type. In the 1941 film directed by Howard Hawks, Ma York epitomizes many of the drudge stereotypes. A widow with three children and hard-to-farm top land, Ma York is shown worshipping, cooking, and working. She rarely speaks, never smiles, has the look of a woman who has lived a long and grueling life, and typifies the sexless maternal figure.[7]

Though, as the title suggests, the film centers on the story of Sgt. Alvin York, of the Cumberland Mountains in Tennessee, it is worth focusing briefly on the role of his mother—if only because of how effectively she typifies the drudge role. In an early scene she walks a long distance to the store in town and returns home only to continue her work as a mother, a cook, and a housekeeper. She sends her youngest son off with food, while she is left without. She is utterly humorless throughout the film, bereft of any semblance of joy. From her drab attire to her hunched walk, she is a drudge of the most prototypical form. This early film establishes firmly the embodiment of the renderings so often reported by journalists and writers who passed through the region.

▶ The Younger Feists

The feist, a hunting dog known for being independent, spunky, energetic, and fierce—even if small—is a central caricature of Appalachian women. The feist has a particular wildness, which can be shown as alluring or as terrifying (such as the goat woman of *Cold Mountain*). Some films manage to show a transformation, while others show a woman who can fit into traditional cultural norms but maintains a particular independent streak that is beloved (Loretta Lynn in *Coalminer's Daughter*; Ella Garth of *Wild River*). These types develop, as most of the others, from a century of portrayals with various connections to reality, but they are caricatured and transformed by Hollywood. The feist is ruthless in her independence, provoking some level of fear from those who misunderstand. The feist has found ways to harness the violence around her and to navigate—like a trickster—the culture that oppresses her. Not completely dissimilar from a male type in Appalachian film that I call the monstrous mountaineer, this figure can at times appear destructive but is more often comic in her representation. Both extreme iterations serve to belittle a strong woman, though there is some space preserved in between that casts Appalachian women as powerful.

The figure of the feist, like other stereotypes taken to extremes, has its basis in earlier representations and a tie to reality. Mountain women have a rich history of labor organizing and fierce independence. The more public one's work, of course, the more recorded her history. In the case of Appalachian women, there is both the domestic work and the more public work that offer models of strong and outspoken women to produce, eventually, cinematic images of women like Norma Rae.

Women of the Mountain South, published in 2016, works to historicize and contextualize the various roles of women whose labor—in and out of the home—gives shape to their lives and to the region. The rich history is conveyed in a complex way in this collection, ranging from female steelworkers to organizers to coal miners. As Connie Park Rice writes in the introduction, "Community activism on all levels has shaped the construction and reconstruction of Appalachian identity and continues to do so today" (Park Rice and Tedesco 2016, 27).

To some extent films have demonstrated the role of female laborers, in part because it supports the image of Appalachian women as drudges. What is also shown, though, is the strength and independence of the mountain women who disrupt norms and fight against the capitalist oppression through sometimes disguised methods. Audiences have space for a female enacting a disruptive femininity when that woman is Appalachian and already alternative and subversive.

Since the first decade of filmmaking, images of wild mountain women have drawn in viewers. In the first four years of film (1908–12), half a dozen films focused on this type—showing the fierce independence of women of the mountains. An early obsession with young mountain women plays on the tension between female vulnerability in the Victorian era and the atypical assertion celebrated in the mountains. In a number of early films (*Bonnie of the Hills*, 1911; *A Mountain Tragedy*, 1912), mountain women are able to effectively wield guns to defend the homestead. This ability seems to come from a life apart from the influences of society and is generally seen as positive. Once the husband returns or awakens, the gun is returned to his hands. The point is not that a mountain woman is violent, but that—if necessary—she can defend herself. Like most characteristics, though, this taken to an extreme produces what Jerry Williamson refers to as a "hellcat." In *Blackened Hills* (1912a; dir. Allan Dwan) both an elder feist, in the form of a mountain witch, and a younger feist are featured. The younger feist functions to tempt the good mountaineer but is eventually defeated. Here the young feist is negatively portrayed, but in more interesting character twists, the hellcat blends with the naive woman of the mountains to produce an alluring, if not heroic, figure. In *Wooers of Mountain Kate* (1912b; dir. Allan Dwan), for example, three men fall in love with a wild woman of the mountains. She appeals to them with her exotic wildness, but eventually she is left to remain as a hermit in the mountains. Mountain Kate needs to be saved from the mountains (as in so many films of the period, including *Madge of the Mountains*, 1911; and *A Blue Ridge Romance*, 1912).[8] Instead, when Mountain Kate stays in the mountains, she claims the space of the other—and is left alone.

Norma Rae

The 1979 Martin Ritt feature, *Norma Rae*, centers on a laborer in a cotton mill in a small southern town. Facing the unfair labor practices that have entrapped her family for at least two generations, with no sign of change for the next generation, Norma Rae (Sally Field) is influenced by a union organizer (Reuben Marshasky, played by Ron Leibman) to join the union and work to unionize the mill. Her biggest challenge is not the textile bosses but her husband, Sonny, who feels that she is spending too much time away from home and family. The truth wins out, though, as Norma Rae shares her life experiences with her kids and Sonny. She continues to work toward a strike and eventually unionizes the factory and even strengthens her bond with her husband (Sonny, played by Beau Bridges).

In name and in topic this is a film about a female laborer. It is also a film about a mother, a lover, a wife, a daughter, and a child of small-town poverty. Norma Rae typifies the sort of strong and defiant Appalachian woman that writers and filmmakers had seen for decades but had tended to portray negatively. Here we see the dangers of factory work. In an early scene Norma Rae's mother, who also works at the mill, becomes temporarily deaf. Norma Rae is enraged, but the local doctor patronizingly says, "She can get another job," prompting an irate Norma Rae to scream the frustrating truth of the moment, "What other job? There ain't no other job in this town!" This reality threatens to grind Norma Rae down, and we see her escape through alcohol and abusive sex in the early parts of the film.

Within the life of the film, Norma Rae's enlightenment comes from labor organizer Reuben Marshasky; the inspiration for the film came from Crystal Lee Sutton, a textile worker at J. P. Stevens Textiles in Roanoke Rapids. The precedent of women like Norma Rae who boldly organize despite cultural and financial pressures to remain complacent are found in histories of Appalachia such as Kiran Bhatraju's *Mud Creek Medicine: The Life of Eula Hall and the Fight for Appalachia* (2013), Jane B. Stephenson's *Courageous Paths: Stories of Nine Appalachian Women* (1996), and Shelly Romalis's *Pistol Packin' Mama: Aunt Molly Jackson and the Politics of Folksong* (1999), to name a few. These determined feists not only changed the ways that their lives played out but created even more space for strong Appalachian women.

In Hollywood cinema some films make light of this determination, while others treat the figures with respect. In the case of *Norma Rae*, there was wide support for the role of this feisty woman, who is called in a *New York*

Times review a "resilient young woman of no great education but a lot of common sense" (Canby 1970). This resilience is praised and earns Norma Rae, the character, renewed hope and a chance to rewrite the script for her hometown. This same resilience and spunk earns *Norma Rae*, the film, a firm place in the American imagining of the southern Appalachian woman who exists outside of the norm but is unafraid to boldly shape the world around her. Again this situates the Appalachian woman as an other, which we see in such films as *Coalminer's Daughter* (1980; dir. Michael Apted) and *Winter's Bone* (2010; dir. Debra Granik).

Nell

This tension between innocence and wildness that vivifies a figure like Norma Rae appears unchecked in the 1994 film *Nell*. The Michael Apted film, starring Jodie Foster in the eponymous role, offers a more contemporary example of the obsession with the feist in the form of extreme and unchecked wilderness. In this film, which earned Jodie Foster a nomination for an Academy Award for Best Actress, a woman is "discovered" living in a primitive cabin after her mother's death. Nell, now a young woman, had been conceived with her twin sister during their mother's rape. Their mother, a recluse, raised them apart from town, based in Robbinsville, North Carolina. Nell and her twin develop a twin code, and when the twin dies as a young girl, Nell's development is seemingly stunted. She is traumatized and isolated when a local therapist finds her, establishes contact with her, and eventually saves her from institutionalization. Along the way he falls in love with the rival therapist; Nell serves as a strange surrogate lover and daughter for the couple.

As a "wild child," Nell draws attention of scientists, journalists, and psychologists precisely because she is unique. She is a reminder of the frontier past and can be traced to early twentieth-century representations of independent mountain people who resist civilization and are shown as superior, but always other. As in other films, like *Songcatcher*, the "native" protagonists are actually in a superior position, and it is civilization that is savage. The plot of *Nell* is contrived and crowds the potentially interesting figure of Nell into a secondary role in the love story that unfolds. Janet Maslin (1994) writes, "Nell ought to occupy center stage in this story, but too much of the time she is relegated to the capacity of pet primitive. There is the terrible feeling that the doctors will be learning valuable lessons from their experience with Nell." This use of Nell as a mountain woman and a young feist shows the vibrance of the uncivilized and the rejuvenating force of the mountains, and ultimately the strange and peculiar land and people of Appalachia.

The film's most compelling moments certainly center on Nell, as the viewer is led into a discovery of her wildness. She is perceived as savage when she lashes out in fear and is sexualized by young boys in the community on her visit to town, but she is ultimately revered as better than her civilized contemporaries. The delivery of this heavy-handed message invited critique from reviewers such as Kenneth Turan (1994), who, writing for the *Los Angeles Times*, called the film unrealistic: "In today's pervasive anti-science, anti-cities environment, all it takes is one vision of natural Nell dancing alone in the luminous moonlight and one glance at Dr. Olsen's officious supervisor (Richard Libertini) to figure out which way this movie has stacked the deck."

Viewers are meant to understand that the wilderness is ideal. It is the wilderness that brings together the two doctors. The wilderness is beautiful and pure and regenerative. The wilderness is a safe harbor, not only for Nell but for others who come to take temporary respite in her woods in the film's final scene. Ultimately, though, even Nell's closest friends go back into town to live their lives. They, like the Atlanta paddlers in *Deliverance*, visit the wilderness but don't join it. In *Nell*, unlike *Deliverance*, the promise of retreat into the wilderness remains. It is this promise that makes the figure of the wilderness woman, one iteration of the feist, so enduring.

Winter's Bone

As scholars like those included in *Women of the Mountain South* work to show, only from an uninformed perspective does the Appalachian woman appear to be a victim. *Winter's Bone* (2010; dir. Debra Granik) conveys the subversive nature of women who are seemingly controlled by a misogynistic culture but who use their wits to thrive in such a setting. A cursory glance at the first half of the film reveals women who are isolated and dependent on vicious men. Ree Dolly (Jennifer Lawrence) is among the most pitiable of figures, until we understand how forcefully she denies pity. Ree is living in poverty with her depressed-beyond-salvation mother, and her father has gone missing. Inspired by the Collins family near author Daniel Woodrell's hometown, the Dolly clan is known for the trouble that they cause. Currently, they are deeply involved in the production and distribution of methamphetamine—crystal meth. They are a terrifying and violent group, bound by ties that are never clear to Ree as she works to navigate her place in this community. Her missing father put up the family plot for bail and fails to appear for court. Now Ree, who takes care of her two younger siblings and her mother, has one week to find her father to keep her home from being repossessed. While this is a search for a man, and the male presence and threat—particularly of Uncle Teardrop—is powerful, it is a story of women who must find their way in a world of violence and kinship.

Ree's friends are unreliable, Ree's mom is dysfunctional, and Ree's aunts seem too fearful to help her. But by the end of the film, it is evident that what may appear to be a man's world is actually controlled by women who are fierce, ingenious, manipulative, and fearless. There is no gentle inner circle that Ree enters, as the women of her family eventually lead her to her father's body. The closest thing to maternalism or kindness occurs when Ree's aunt forces her to hold the waterlogged and decaying hand of her drowned father as the aunt revs up the chainsaw and cuts through the bone herself. Ree is spared that indignity, but to call the action "kind" is a stretch. Considering the context, though, kindness takes various shapes, and the abduction at gunpoint that leaves Ree in a boat with the cold, dead hand of her father is among the most generous acts of the plot. These women, who seem first to belong to the world that Raine described—silent, sinewy laborers who kept quiet and were victims of a cruel world of poverty and male dominance—may in fact be the underworld matriarchs. Perhaps the drudge is the creation of outsiders, shaped of empathy but also inability to fully see the world into which they were looking.

Ree not only exists in a culture that works her hard and rewards her little; she has found ways to navigate the dark realms that limit her opportunities— wandering into spaces where she is not invited, but using the violence around her as a way to succeed. Rather than actively perpetrating violence, Ree exists alongside violence. Her definition depends on that violence.

The Elder Feist

One iteration of the feist is disempowered by her age. To show a fierce woman that is less threatening, the granny type was popularized. In *The Southern Highlander and His Homeland*, John Campbell acknowledges the unique position of Appalachian women, paying particular attention to the unexpected power of the grannies. Campbell's observations demonstrate the respect that they have earned with their age. The granny "has gained a freedom and a place of irresponsible authority in the home hardly rivaled by any man in the family. Her grown sons pay to her an attention *which they do not always accord their wives*; and her husband, while he remains still undisputed master of the home, defers to her opinion to a degree unknown in her younger days. Her daughters and her grandchildren she frankly rules" (1921, 140–41; emphasis mine).

Literary depictions and sociological and historical studies of grannies show a deep respect for female Appalachian elders. This respect is demonstrated in dramatic films, such as *Cold Mountain*, *Wild River*, and *Foxfire* but veers to the comedic in earlier films like *Sargent York* and takes a caricatured turn in comedic settings like *The Beverly Hillbillies*. The basis for each of these iterations is likely an accurate if generalized image of Appalachian grannies, who are straight talkers of few words, whose wisdom is lived rather than academic, and who demand a level of respect within the family. In some arenas these traits are taken seriously and represented in a romanticized way. In others these same traits are threatening and become fodder for comic scenes. The lack of "book smarts" shows up, as Mammy Yokum can't recall how many children she has. The strength and assertion becomes a gun-toting Granny Clampett.

Mary Ella Engel writes, "So persistent is this characterization of elderly mountain women that the mountain 'Granny' has become a stock image in American popular culture, a staple on television shows like 'The Beverly Hillbillies,' in which irascible Granny Clampett dispensed both folk wisdom and physical correction in equal measure" (2010, 211). While there is overlap between the perception and lived experiences in some cases, the goal of this work is to parse out the differences to understand the investment in particular images.

Sally Ward Maggard's (1999) Mae and granny figures are more similar than they are disparate. Both are used for comic relief, and neither is meant to be taken as a full person. Scanning the earliest depictions of Appalachia, one finds the background filled with buffoonish grannies and the foreground with men fighting over outlandish Maes.

The granny figure appeared with some consistency in silent early films but was solidified by the 1940s. In the 1925 silent film *Ma Cagle of Sun-Up*, the protagonist is old-fashioned, intent on carrying out family revenge. She is seen as outdated throughout the film and eventually concedes power when her son becomes sheriff rather than pursuing vigilante justice. Over the next two decades, Mammy Yokum and Ma Kettle emerged and became recognizable figures, affirming the type of the mountain granny. Alfred Gerald Caplin, a Latvian American from Connecticut, using the nom de plume Al Capp, developed a comic strip titled *Li'l Abner*, which entered syndication in 1934. A decade later a series of popular films beginning in 1947 with *The Egg and I* came to be known as Ma and Pa Kettle films, produced and directed by Chester Erskine. A generation later, in 1962, the granny figure was revitalized in the role of Granny Clampett in the Paul Henning television program, *The Beverly Hillbillies*. Each of these forms of entertainment provides a consistent image of a granny figure who is fierce but ignorant, unintentionally comedic, hardworking but ineffective, maternal but not warm. The continued presence of a mountain granny from 1934 to 1971 both shaped and reflected the general perception of mountain elders. The mountain granny, like the similar African American mammy, is a caricature that both distances the viewer from the subject on screen and creates a vaguely comforting and nonthreatening image of mountain women.

One strain that appears in most granny vehicles is the ineffective homemaker. Whether at home, as in the case of Dogpatch and the Kettles, or in a new environment, like Granny Clampett's California, the granny is shown to belong to a time and place that is always past its prime. Even in the new and fancy kitchen in Hollywood, Granny Clampett boils herbs and greens in the pots she brought with her. Similarly, Ma and Pa Kettle live in disarray and misunderstand the world around them. In an episode called "Second Hand Underwear," from 1949, in nearly any scene one could select, these characteristics are made evident. Ma is disheveled, wearing a flour sack as an apron, with loosely bound hair. She is not made to be attractive in her attire or her carriage. As she sets the table, she simply pushes into the floor anything in the way of the plates. She is the matriarch, raising fifteen kids and taking care of a foolish husband. Ma Kettle is hardly a hero, though. She is too much a caricature of ignorance, backwardness, and slovenly housekeeping to step into the role of the protagonist. Although she laughs often, we are laughing *at* Ma Kettle, not *with* her.

Yet there is more to this granny type in some circumstances. Superficially, Mammy Yokum seems to function like her contemporary, Ma Kettle, and her subsequent type, Granny Clampett, as a fool. Anyone who has read or watched these representations of the granny knows, though, that there is more to each of these women than her foolishness. Mammy Yokum emerges as the moral voice, Granny Clampett reveals the stupidity of those "civilized folks" around her as often as she makes a fool of herself, and Ma Kettle grounds her family as they adjust to a changing world. According to Thomas Inge and Edwin T. Arnold, Mammy Yokum is given space in her "o-ray-shuns" to serve as the moral voice. Whether it is about "the importance of safeguarding the freedom" in 1949, as Inge makes evident (2001, 8), or the development of an open mind, on which Arnold focuses, Mammy Yokum was at once serving as comic relief and fulfilling the Victorian ideals of femininity as the morally upright woman. Arnold explains,

> On New Year's Day 1947, [Capps] had Mammy Yokum lecture America on racial and ethnic discrimination, and the comparison she used was striking. She reminded Abner's readers of the handicapped soldiers "whose laigs an eyes an innards we had to use up durin the late lamented (espeshly by our enemies') war." Then she drew an analogy to the "other handy-capped youngsters we seem to of forgot about; them which is handy-capped by bein' of a little diffrunt race than most of us, or a diffrunt way of worshippin, mebbe." . . . In either case, race or religion, these people were "outsiders," different from "most of us," and thus in a very real way "consumable." (1997, 428)

Ultimately, I find that even with a more complex set of types and even with more serious treatment of Appalachian women, there is a truth to the idea that mountain women are understood in an intermediary place—in that tension—between types.

In 1981, when Sidney Saylor Farr collected and annotated more than a thousand sources referencing Appalachian women, she divided her findings in a dozen subheadings, or frames, ranging from "Coal Mining" to "Music" to "Religion and Folklore."[9] Scholars have tried to understand the gender roles in Appalachia variously; Melissa Latimer and Ann M. Oberhauser offer a statistical analysis to demonstrate, for example, the ways that "dynamic gender relations affect the diverse experiences of men and women in Appalachia's economic development" (2004, 269). Others have looked at the outspoken women of Appalachia in portraits of particular women (see Romalis 1999; Stephenson 1996; and Norris and Cyprès 1996). While political scientist Karen Beckwith (1998) frames women as part of "collective identities" within movements like the Pittston Coal Strike, Shannon Elizabeth Bell (2013) collects interviews with central Appalachian women fighting for environmental justice. Anthropologist Mary Anglin revisits the idea of the "backtalking woman" who helps us see a "problematized Appalachia, an Appalachia wherein the residues of local color reflect an ongoing struggle over identity and power relations, and not an uncomplicated version of America's past" so that we "understand that regional identity, that selective fiction, is contested ground" (1992, 112). Both Katherine Kelleher Sohn (2006) and Erica Abrams Locklear (2011) study Appalachian women's literacy practices—the first through primary interviews with eight Appalachian women and the latter through analysis of literary depictions of women's literacy. Danny L. Miller (1996) offers reflections on Appalachian women in fiction, while Joyce Dyer (1998) collects the voices of Appalachian women writers as they reflect on place. Individually, each snapshot of Appalachian women comes into focus and presents a framed shot. We know where to settle our eyes. We understand the image. Stepping closer to the image of Appalachian women, though, reveals that just outside of the frame or somewhere in the background is antithetical evidence that complicates the image.

Women in Appalachia have generally experienced the same range of opportunities and limitations as women throughout the rest of the nation. The aforementioned scholars expose that range of experiences through focused studies, making evident that some women are limited by a lack of education, some women are vocal in the labor movement, and some women are in positions to lead their families and to speak up in their community. The same might be said of a close look at women in many pockets of America and across the globe.[10] The work of scholars like Abrams, Anglin, Beckwith, Latimer and Oberhauser, Miller, and Sohn is to explore what is particularly Appalachian about these trends and moments in history. Their work thrives on the finite understanding of particular women, evaluating trends in narrowly defined parameters and drawing larger logical conclusions. I hope to do the same work, adding my own voice to this chorus as I work to understand the stakes of representation of Appalachian women in film.

A paucity of images of women is a contributor to the narrow typing that limits full representation of women. In "'Beyond the Mountains': The Paradox of Women's Place in Appalachian History," Barbara Ellen Smith offers a complicated reading of her subject. Reflecting on the narrative of her own grandmother, who links Smith to the mountains but who, herself, hated the mountains, Smith moves broadly to see the ways that individuals and fields of studies simplify or ignore the complex and contradictory roles and characteristics of Appalachian women. It is, Smith argues, this complexity that leads to a looking away from women in scholarship and representation. The limited perspective that frames traditional narratives about the region focuses on male figures: "Generic 'mountaineers,' 'settler,' and 'Appalachian'— most of them implicitly male—crowd the pages of the classic texts on the region. Fashioned from Adam's rib, 'mountain women' are secondary, entirely compatible with the 'mountain men' from whom they are derived" (1999, 2). Rather than acknowledging the involvement of women in labor strikes and the power of women in their own homes alongside the unequal experience of poverty for women, the tension of reality falls out of the frame, leaving symbolic and silenced figures.

Whether it is negative representation or a lack of representation, the effect on self-image is evident. In *Whistlin' and Crowin' Women of Appalachia*, a study of the literary practices of women of Appalachia, Katherine Kelleher Sohn writes about the ways that stereotypes—mostly notable illiteracy or lack of intelligence—impact the feelings of the women featured in her study. Despite the women's actions, the perception of inability prevails. The women she has interviewed demonstrate the range of lived experiences in the region, but all are impacted by the stereotypes that follow them. In a discussion of one of her subjects, Sohn reflects, "What cries out to me is her continued definition of herself as a poor reader when she reads nursing journals, the Internet, and complex medical books well enough to pass certification exams. Like Lucy, Jean cannot believe that she is a good reader because of her narrow definition of reading as relating only to novels when, in fact, many would see her choice of reading medical tomes over Harlequin romances a superior one" (2006, 115). The idea that Jean should be a poor reader because of where she is raised is stronger than the evidence that she is something different.

If the diversity of women leads to a lack of clear perception, as Smith (1999) argues, or a misperception, as in Sohn (2006), the impact of stereotyping on self-perception and identity is very real indeed. The reach of a study on stereotyping and representation—whether in film, media, or literature—is immediate and extensive. To piece apart the ways that women are shown in film is to delve into the cultural value placed on women, the expectations guiding them, and the motivation for such images. To study the ways women are represented is to study the ways that women live—and are expected to live. Perception determines performance, as Sohn's subjects make clear.

Notes

INTRODUCTION

1. I am using the term *other* as it has been taken up in literary and film theory, with its basis in Jacques Lacan's (1997) self-other dichotomy. Lacan argued that to situate a definition of self there must be an other from which we understand ourselves to be distinct. Edward Said's (1978) use of *other* is derived more directly from Jacques Derrida's (1971) concept of alterity. For Said, othering stabilizes the West as normative and depends on the other for this stability.

2. Selected works on African American representation in film include the following: Baldwin (1976); Bogle (2001); Cripps (1993, 1977); and hooks (1996). See also the selected works on Native American representation in film: Bird (1996); Buscombe (2006); Herzberg (2008); and Kilpatrick (1999).

3. The Blue Collar Comedy Tour that helped launch the careers of comedians such as Larry the Cable Guy (Daniel Whitney) by building on the comedy of writer Lewis Grizzard and comedian Jeff Foxworthy is interestingly sold to the very audience that it seems to ridicule. This claiming of an identity that had been used as an insult became incredibly popular. While an ownership of working-class status offers the potential to subvert the power of derogatory terms by using them (as has been seen with terms like "queer"), there is an uncritical affirmation of negative stereotypes that can also take place in such a set up.

4. At boutiques throughout the South, one can find GRITS printed on T-shirts, hand towels, and serving trays. Girls Raised in the South typifies the sort of uncritical praise of southern identity popularized by Lewis Grizzard and others.

5. The *Appalachian Region Borders* map appears to have been drawn for teaching purposes by David E. Whisnant (n.d.), University of North Carolina at Chapel Hill professor emeritus of English. In his collection, held at university's Chapel Hill

Library in Collection 20071-z, is a link to the compilation map. Appalachian State University features a link to the library in the Appalachian Collection's website ("W.L. Eury Appalachian Collection" 2017). The original link can be found at "Southern Folklife Collection" (2017).

6. Regional studies takes up this issue broadly. Southern studies, for example, responds to similar frustrations at monolithic depictions of a vast region. In her article, "When Strangers Bring Their Cameras: The Poetics and Politics of Othered Places," Cameron draws an explicit connection between Maine and Kentucky.

7. In *Appalachia: A History*, J. Williams writes, "Frost was assisted by a former student who had become a professional geologist, C. Willard Hayes." Even as this team set out to draw firm boundaries, when 194 counties "did not follow geological features precisely," they were still included. His naming the region "Southern Highlands" rather than "Southern Appalachians" reveals his somewhat subjective interest in the cultural definitions of place and place markers (2002, 12).

8. Campbell writes, rather poetically, "The traveler who follows the trails of this far country, fords its rushing streams, and forces his way through thickets of rhododendron and laurel to rest on some beech-shaded bank of moss, and who toward sunset checks his horse on the ridge to trace the thread of smoke which signals welcome, may yet be at a loss for a name to describe the land; but when at dawn he wakes with mist rising from every cove and valley, and echoes still sounding of half-remembered traditions, folk-lore and folk-songs, recited or sung before the fire by 'granny' or 'grandpap,' he knows there is but one name that will do it justice—the Southern Highlands" (1921, 12).

9. The Appalachian Regional Commission was established by Congress in 1965 as a part of an economic-development plan. Today the commission lists the following five objectives on its website: "(1) Economic Opportunities; (2) Ready Workforce; (3) Critical Infrastructure; (4) Natural and Cultural Assets; and (5) Leadership and Community Capacity" ("About ARC," n.d.).

10. Blauch (1975) outlines various opinions in his work: in 1861 Arnold Guyot's division of Appalachia into "Northern" and "Southern"; the extension of the southern boundary into central Alabama by W. J. McGee in 1891; a new definition in 1902 in a report to Theodore Roosevelt drawn by rivers on the western border; an extension of the Cumberland Plateau in 1937 by E. Lucy Braun in 1937 based on "floristics"; and further divisions of "Northern," "Middle," and "Southern" in 1960 by Robinson. This snapshot offers evidence of the contentious nature of the very methods of defining the region.

11. The Ozarks, while not considered Appalachia by many maps and not a part of the Appalachian range, are included in this study. There is a precedent in Appalachian studies for including the Ozarks, particularly when it comes to studies of Appalachian types and representation of the region. For example, Harkins (2004) includes the Ozarks for these same reasons in his discussion of the hillbilly and Sut Lovingood figures.

12. Inscoe and Satterwhite are among scholars currently at work on books on Appalachian film. Inscoe's focus is Civil War–era representation, while Satterwhite

is focusing on the horror genre. Williamson's aforementioned texts (1994, 1995a) set the stage for this ongoing conversation, of course.

13. In *The Making and Unmaking of Whiteness* (2001), editors Rasmussen, Nexica, Wray, and Klinenberg outline the following definitions of whiteness that shape their collection: "Whiteness Is Invisible and Unmarked," "Whiteness Is 'Empty' and White Identity Is Established through Appropriation," "Whiteness Is Structural Privilege," "Whiteness Is Violence and Terror," and "Critical Whiteness Studies Is an Antiracist Practice" (10–13).

14. Housed in the W. L. Eury Appalachian Collection at Appalachian State University, Williamson's (1995b) catalog of *Southern Mountaineers Filmography* currently exists as a static list of annotated films that Williamson curated. I am gradually transitioning that list into a dynamic and searchable catalog, which will also be available through Appalachian State University's website.

15. Indeed, an issue of *Appalachian Journal* (vol. 10, nos. 1–2) is devoted entirely to the topic of "Whiteness and Racialization in Appalachia."

16. Eller writes, "We *know* Appalachia exists because we need it to exist in order to define what we are not" (2008, 3), echoing Baldwin's assertion that "no one was white before he/she came to America. It took generations and a vast amount of coercion, before this became a white country" (2010, 136).

17. "The Mirror Stage as Formative of the Function of the I as Revealed in Psychoanalytic Experience" was presented at the Sixteenth International Congress of Psychoanalysis in Zurich on July 17, 1949. It was later translated and published in *Social Theory: The Multicultural Readings* (Lacan 2010).

18. Lacan's writing during the 1930s and 1940s informs my approach to the impact of cinema on identity and power. Tamise Van Pelt writes of Lacan's 1949 paper, "This essay presents a developmental portrait of the child's entry into language, an event that irremediably splits the child into a speaking subject (a *je*) decentered from an ideal ego (*moi*) whose unattainable image of perfection the child narcissistically wishes to find reflected by others, especially the mother" (1997, 59).

19. *Nell* (1994), discussed in chapter 3, portrays the Wild Mountain Child, while the popular television series *Christy* offers an idealized view of what William Goodell Frost (1899) called "our contemporary ancestors." In my conversation with photographer Stacy Kranitz, discussed in the final chapter, Kranitz explained that she fell in love with the region by watching this show. She photographs herself *as* Christy in her series on Appalachia (Huntington, W.Va., March 29, 2014).

20. Scholars such as Bogle (2001), Rhines (1996), Guerrero (1993), and hooks (1996) have chronicled the relationship between white filmmakers, black characters, and white audiences.

CHAPTER 1. Hillbilly as American Indian

1. In *Elements*, Clabough notes that the original manuscript for *Deliverance* contains marginalia, in which Dickey wrote as he conceived of the rapists, "perhaps escaped convicts" (2002, 38).

2. In one scene in *Winter's Bone*, to prove her father's death, Ree must bring back part of his arm, which she removes from his drowned body with a chainsaw—under the watch of the "kind" women of the community who have learned to adapt to the extreme mistreatment and misogyny of their culture by enacting their own forms of control.

3. The following films feature southern, but not Appalachian, settings: Walter Hill's *Southern Comfort* (1981), Tobe Hooper's *Deathtrap/Eaten Alive* (1977), and Jeff Lieberman's *Just before Dawn* (1981).

4. The deep and historical culture of Native Americans has been chronicled since John Smith and William Bartram. John Smith, in *The Generall Historie of Virginia* (1624), collects "facts" about various inhabitants of seventeenth-century America, presenting the land for vicarious European readers. The emphasis on the barbarism and inherent violence of the Indians justifies their removal and genocide, based on the idea that savages, while they may well have some quaint traditions, cannot be civilized and are thus doomed to extinction. In the eighteenth century Thomas Jefferson (1787) continued the ambivalent treatment of Indians, even as he benefited from their displacement. As Deloria (1998) points out, the American Revolution and the Boston Tea Party in particular demonstrate white America's use of the conceptual Indian to insert savagery into civilization, as the white Tea Partiers participated in an act of civil disobedience dressed as Mohawks.

5. For a full discussion of both Roosevelt and the Boy Scout movement in the context of overcivilization, see Bederman (1995).

6. In a less flattering reading of *Deliverance*, Heilbrun writes of this dichotomous order: "Ed has fled with his buddies into the world of the American movie fantasy where it's 'either him or us,' where the need to kill is conveniently unavoidable, where murder and violence and the homosexual rape he calls 'a kind of love' are all that can be mustered up in opposition to the 'long declining routine of our lives'" (1994, 60).

7. Importantly, Cora is biracial in Cooper's *The Last of the Mohicans*. Cora's mother, whom Colonel Munro married, is the daughter of an island slave and white "gentleman." As Munro explains to Heyward, "There it was my lot to form a connection with one who in time became my wife and the Mother of Cora. She was the daughter of a gentleman of those isles, by a lady whose misfortune it was, if you will," said the old man proudly, "to be descended, remotely, from that unfortunate class who are so basely enslaved to administer to the wants of a luxurious people" (Cooper 2003, 187–88). In Mann's film, Cora's multiraciality is only implied but never explicitly stated. The casting of Daniel Day-Lewis as Hawkeye and Madeleine Stowe as Cora does support the reading that both figures are somehow liminal, visually associated by their similar long dark hair.

8. Lindborg, in his reading of these scenes, asserts, "But behind this merging of fantasy and fact, there remains a continuing sense of the dream, of unreality, of play-acting. . . . 'We were all acting it out,' [Ed] repeats later. In spite of his wish to return home, he recognizes that they are 'cast in roles' and must carry them out" (1974, 87). The theme of overcivilization as a threat to masculinity, or what Butler calls the "impotence of the civilized," has its roots in the earliest American texts and has provided

a rich area of study for scholars (1976, 121). Richard Slotkin's *Regeneration through Violence* (1973) offers an early reading of the prevalence of "city boys" to return to a primitive state—often in a wilderness setting untouched by civilization and frequently in interaction with Native Americans—to connect to their primal manliness. The nineteenth-century "disease" of neurasthenia, the legitimized male version of hysteria, was born of overcivilization, according to George Miller Beard, who legitimized and named the disorder. The treatment for hysteria was solitary rest; the treatment for neurasthenia was a trip into the wilderness. Daniel Carter Beard, founder of the Boy Scouts of America, and Teddy Roosevelt, victim of neurasthenia, both celebrated the treatment, which called for weak city boys to get outside, hunt, and revisit the primal instincts that the city had all but erased. Roosevelt's costuming as an Indian, as he rebuilt his image as a Rough Rider and as a man's man, offers a concrete nineteenth-century visual image of the assessment of overcivilization as weak and effeminate.

9. First, General Webb makes and immediately breaks a deal with the colonial militia—promising that they may return to defend their homesteads if necessary and then denying that promise despite the report of a murdered family. Colonel Munro shows himself to be inconsiderate of the colonial and Indian allies, as well as an ineffective military leader who surrenders to the French. Finally, the French leader General Montcalm honorably offers retreat to the Munro but then covertly encourages Maqua, his Indian ally-assassin, to lead an attack on the retreating British.

10. After witnessing the rampaged farm of colonials, which should prompt the British army to send the militia back to protect their homes, Duncan deceitfully denies what he saw. This breach of trust pushes Cora to finally and definitively refuse Duncan's repeated proposal of marriage. In further scenes, while he and the Munro daughters have been captured by the Hurons, his dependence on the Mohicans for survival marks him as even weaker than Cora, who knows enough to leave a trail for their eventual rescuers.

11. Bobby reads here as inconsiderate and self-centered, as he walks confidently about the yard and even refers to a rusted-out car as "mine," recalling his sexual adventures in the backseat of his car of the same model. His ownership of the car extends to his condescending treatment of the locals. Bobby rarely speaks directly to the locals, but instead speaks about them when he says, "Lewis, we got a live one here."

12. Trevor Jones and Randy Edelman scored the music for the film, which was originally to be electronic. Director Michael Mann believed that the film needed a more "epic" soundtrack that electronic music could not capture, and this collaboration was born.

13. Steele, in his review of *The Last of the Mohicans* for the *Journal of American History*, points out, "In reality, Munro and all the other British officers survived the attack unharmed" (1993, 1180).

14. In both the earlier scene at the gas station and this scene in the woods, it is interesting that the action takes place outside. At the station Ed and Lewis stand in the doorway of a shop, and the camera shoots from within, whereas in the rape scene, all action is unenclosed. The entrapment, in both scenes, is psychological more than physical. Certainly, in the rape scene the shotgun is a physical force used to trap

Bobby and Ed, but leading up to that moment Boorman demonstrates the strange encounter shifting into a dangerous encounter with editing, camera angles, and framing. In short, he creates a sense of enclosure even in the openness of the outdoors.

15. As Clabough reads the scene, "Small, lost and deprived of his masculinity, Ed describes his language as 'clinging to the city' . . . wholly unable to adjust his tactics to the situation in which he finds himself" (2002, 53–54). In this moment Ed and Bobby are of the city while the rapists are in their element, comfortable and knowledgeable. Nevertheless, on a continuum of urbanity/vulnerability and wilderness/safety, Ed is positioned differently and fares better than does Bobby.

16. The second perpetrator, who is here the onlooker as his friend rapes Bobby, is shown as toothless in this scene. After Ed kills a man that he assumes is this perpetrator, he is terrified to see that he has teeth. In a particularly disgusting moment, a horrified Ed—facing his own violent potential and the concept that he may have killed the wrong man—reaches in and confirms that the teeth are false. While it creates an intense moment of suspense, I maintain questions about the likelihood that this man, first, would have a relatively expensive dental bridge and, second, after witnessing the death of his companion, would go home to retrieve the bridge before avenging his death.

17. The sheriff was played by James Dickey, arguably as a compromise to get him out of the way of the filming. According to Christopher Dickey's book *Summer of Deliverance*, the author was inserting himself and creating problems with Boorman's direction. He left town for a while, with the promise that he would return to play the part of the sheriff.

18. In fact, Lewis struggles to find the river, causing one of the Griner brothers to joke, "It ain't nothing but the biggest fuckin' river in the state."

CHAPTER 2. Appalachian Woman as Mammy

1. "Rocky Top," written by Felice and Boudreaux Bryant, was popularized in 1967 by the Osborne Brothers, when it was released on the Decca/MCA label.

2. Importantly, the intention of authors like Stowe is not necessarily the same as the eventual impact. As a type, though, the mammy came to represent a nonthreatening, desexualized, loyal presence who would fight even black Union soldiers to protect the white master's home.

3. Although the Reconstruction Act of 1867 ensured male suffrage for black men and forced the five military districts in the South to uphold the U.S. Constitution, by 1876 these governments were weak. As Goings explains it, "by 1876 the temporary experience of democracy was over" (1994, 3). In its place, Goings argues, was the Ku Klux Klan.

4. While a discussion of the differences in these types would be productive, here I use them interchangeably, based on the overlapping and common descriptions that Bogle (2001) and Goings (1994) offer. Bogle uses "Coon," while Goings uses "Sambo."

5. Bogle (2001) mentions, but leaves unresolved, the fact that the casting in *Our Gang* called for a child that could play a boy or girl. Farina was played by Allen Clay-

ton Hoskins and was interchangeably male and female. I, too, must leave this curious fact unresolved, but I link it to the emasculation of male figures and defeminizing of females during this era.

6. Stepin Fetchit is a complex figure, much like Hattie McDaniel, whose roles beg questions of responsibility. Was it Fetchit who demeaned himself by playing into a caricature, or was McDaniel right when she said to a critic, "Why should I complain about making seven thousand dollars a week playing a maid? If I didn't, I'd be making seven dollars a week actually being one!" (Bogle 2001, 82).

7. Maria St. John offers a reading of this feeding scene, in which she argues that it is tied to a breast-feeding scene between Mammy and Scarlett. St. John explains, "the battle is over the locus of control of Scarlett's insides. Mammy's moment of victory consists in her sneakily revealing that she knows what Scarlett has congratulated herself for concealing—her secret, sexual wish. Scarlett maintains the upper hand throughout most of the scene by means of her refusal of food." Eventually, though, Mammy tells Scarlett that she will be "eatin' like a field hand" by the afternoon, and Scarlett eats (1999, 134).

8. Inman, played by Jude Law, is Ada's love interest. He is away from Cold Mountain, fighting in the Civil War.

CHAPTER 3. Mountain Migrant as Mexican Migrant

1. Several well-researched studies of the process of Appalachian migration and the experiences of Appalachian migrants have been published, including, Schwarzweller, Brown, and Mangalam (1971); Philliber and McCoy (1981); Obermiller and Philliber (2017); and Borman and Obermiller (1994). C. Berry (2000) provides the broadest historical account of Appalachian migration.

2. This *Chicago Tribune* set of stories offers a keen insight into the range of experiences and perceptions of Appalachians in Chicago in the late 1960s, just as Haskell Wexler was filming *Medium Cool*. The letters to the editor following and responding to this series reveals public sentiment as well. Letters from October 20 show the varied responses to the influx of Appalachian migrants. One letter writer defends Appalachians by saying that they are hardworking—language used a few decades later to generalize and defend Latino workers. Another writer remembers the "clean" uptown of her past, subtly describing the Appalachian enclaves as changed and dirty.

3. See also Mendible (2007), whose collection, deeply rooted in feminist and critical race theory, offers optimistic readings of the reimagined Latina body.

4. This scene deserves more attention than I am able to give it in this book. Protagonist John Cassellis attempts to capture a "human interest" story by interviewing an African American cab driver who had made the news due to a good deed. When Cassellis enters his apartment, he is met by relatively militant blacks who chastise him for his inability to hear the stories around him. These were actors and activists arranged by Studs Terkel, who helped with casting and introductions in Chicago. The scene is partially scripted but also allows for improvisation. They explicitly criticize Cassellis for his role in perpetuating racist stereotypes as a journalist.

5. The filmmakers of *Salt of the Earth*, some of whom were members of the Communist Party, were red-listed after the production of the film, which was hardly shown due to the controversy over the politics of the filmmakers. *Medium Cool* earned an *X* rating until 1970, when it was changed to an *R*. Although there is nudity in the fictional segments of the film, the actual language ("Fuck the pigs") heard in the protests surrounding the Democratic National Convention held in Chicago during filming contributed to the original X rating. In later interviews, including one shown in the special features of the Criterion release of *Medium Cool*, Wexler (2013) calls it a "political X rating."

6. (Male) workers picketed from October 1950 to June 1951 and were replaced by their wives, who picketed until January 21, 1952. This information is chronicled on the Global Nonviolent Action Database; see Hameed (2013).

CHAPTER 4. Appalachia and Documentary

1. Joe and Karen Mulloy, Alan and Margaret McSurely, and Anne and Carle Braden were all charged with sedition (Hanna 1998, 376).

2. Herdman cites Aufderheide (2007, 63–64), for this perspective on response to public-affairs films.

3. In his article "Survival and Resistance: Appalshop's First 40 Years," Rend Smith (2008) explains this mobility: "Though it would be considered cumbersome by modern standards, in 1971 the camera offered its wielder something no other camera did: mobility. Here was a chance to walk the streets of a small coal town and ask people what they thought of the Vietnam War; here was the freedom to trek up steep, lush inclines of Kentucky wilderness to roll footage on an expert dulcimer player."

4. In retrospect, Herb Smith recalls the early Appalshop days as overtly political. A teenager who became involved early with Bill Richardson, Smith remembers, "By connecting to the traditional culture of the Appalachian region, we were opting out of the military-industrial machine that was bombing peasants in Southeast Asia" (R. Smith 2008).

5. According to the film, this five-screen projection system was the inspiration for IMAX.

6. Before creating *Hollow*, McMillion Sheldon directed a post-Katrina documentary about the Ninth Ward and a documentary about police brutality.

APPENDIX. Appalachian Types in Cinema

1. At the time of the writing of this book, I know of two other books in progress on Appalachian film. Emily Satterwhite is at work on a book tentatively called *Hillbilly Horror*, and John Inscoe is writing *Appalachia on Film: History, Hollywood, and the Highland South*.

2. According to legend, William Faulkner had a few books that he kept on his bedside shelf throughout his life, and George Washington Harris's *Sut Lovingood* was among them.

3. Ballard cites Thomas Inge here, who credits Sut as the model of Snuffy. According to Ballard, though, Snuffy became more comic when Billy de Beck's assistant, Fred Lasswell, took over (1999, 144). See Billings, Norman, and Ledford (1999) for a fuller discussion of Sut Lovingood.

4. The fact that Emily Satterwhite is covering this topic is a blessing, not only because she is a scholar of great purpose and detail, but also because it gives me an excuse to not watch too many horror films.

5. Williamson (1995a) provides a careful catalog and analysis of these hillbilly images in the opening of his book *Hillbillyland*.

6. Harkins is writing specifically about *Stark Love*, a film that claimed to treat seriously the challenges of mountain life. Despite his lack of knowledge of the region, Karl Brown, writer and director, told Horace Kephart, "I want to show these people as they are. As they *really* are. As human beings, not caricatures" (qtd. in Harkins 2004, 150).

7. Ma York comes close to a smile when, after being struck by lightning, her son Alvin York enters the church and finds salvation.

8. Several of these early films are difficult to access and are known only through reputation. In some cases names of directors are unknown. My knowledge of these films is due to Jerry Williamson's *Southern Mountaineers Filmography* (1995b).

9. Farr's (1981) annotated bibliography, published by the University of Kentucky Press, provides an excellent guide through 150 years of references to Appalachian women. Farr is careful to be fair in her inclusions, not eliminating the negative portrayals of women, to create a full image of the stories that have been told about Appalachian women.

10. In the introduction to her annotated bibliography, Sidney Saylor Farr writes, "For a hundred years and more the Appalachian woman has been exhibited in many different settings, illuminated with different shadings of light, and extolled or criticized. She has been depicted as beautiful and ugly, weak and strong, young and old, a follower, a leader, a homemaker, an activist—depending upon which particular voice one hears and which picture one sees. But the same thing can be said about women the world over—Jewish, Irish, Puerto Rican, Greek. It depends on one's perspective" (1981, xiii).

References

"About ARC." n.d. Appalachian Regional Commission. Accessed November 20, 2017. www.arc.gov/about/index.asp.

Abrams Locklear, Erica. 2011. *Negotiating a Perilous Empowerment: Appalachian Women's Literacies*. Athens: Ohio University Press.

Aigner, Hal. 1972–73. Review of *Deliverance*. *Film Quarterly* 26 (2): 39–41.

Anderson, Benedict. 1983. *Imagined Communities*. London: Verso.

Anglin, Mary. 1992. "A Question of Loyalty: National and Regional Identity in Narratives of Appalachia." *Anthropological Quarterly* 65 (3): 105–16.

Anzaldúa, Gloria. 1987. *Borderlands/La Frontera*. San Francisco: Spinsters Books.

"Appalachian Identity: A Roundtable Discussion." 2010. *Appalachian Journal* 38 (1): 56–76.

"Appalshop's Mission." 2016. Appalshop. Accessed November 20, 2017. www .appalshop.org/about-us/our-mission/.

Apted, Michael. 1980. *Coalminer's Daughter*. Universal City, Calif: Universal Pictures.

———, dir. 1994. *Nell*. Century City, Calif.: Twentieth Century Fox.

Arnold, Edwin T. 1997. "Abner Unpinned: Al Capp's Lil Abner." *Appalachian Journal* 24 (4): 420–36.

Arnow, Harriette. 1954. *The Dollmaker*. New York: Macmillan.

Aufderheide, Pat. 2007. *Documentary Film: A Very Short Introduction*. London: Oxford University Press.

Backes, Clarence. 1968. "The Promised Land Often Looks a Little Grim by the Light of Day." *Chicago Tribune*, September 22, 1968, 430–35.

Baldwin, James. 1976. *The Devil Finds Work*. New York: Dial.

———. 2010. "On Being White and Other Lies." In *The Cross of Redemption: Uncollected Writings*, edited by Randall Kenan, 135–38. New York: Pantheon.

Ballard, Sandra. 1999. "Where Did Hillbillies Come From?" In Billings, Norman, and Ledford 1999, 138–52.

Barcus, Holly R., and Stanley D. Brunn. 2009. "Towards a Typology of Mobility and Place Attachment in Rural America." *Journal of Appalachian Studies* 15, nos. 1–2 (Spring and Fall): 26–48.

Barret, Elizabeth, dir. 2000. *Stranger with a Camera*. Whitesburg, Ky.: Appalshop.

Bataille, Gretchen M., and Charles L. P. Silet, eds. 1980. *The Pretend Indians: Images of Native Americans in the Movies*. Ames: Iowa State University Press.

Batteau, Allen W. 1990. *The Invention of Appalachia*. Tucson: University of Arizona Press.

Beckwith, Karen. 1998. "Collective Identities of Class and Gender: Working-Class Women in the Pittston Coal Strike." *Political Psychology* 19 (1): 147–67.

Bederman, Gail. 1995. *Manliness and Civilization: A Cultural History of Gender and Race in the United States: 1880–1917*. Chicago: University of Chicago Press.

Bell, Shannon Elizabeth. 2013. *Our Roots Run Deep as Ironweed: Appalachian Women and the Fight for Environmental Justice*. Urbana: University of Illinois Press.

Berry, Alec. 2013. "The Hollow: A Documentary Film Project Gives Hope to People in McDowell County." *West Virginia Living*, Spring 2013. www.wvliving.com.

Berry, Chad. 2000. *Southern Migrants, Northern Exiles*. Urbana: University of Illinois Press.

Bhatraju, Kiran. 2013. *Mud Creek Medicine: The Life of Eula Hall and the Fight for Appalachia*. Louisville, Ky.: Butler Books.

Biberman, Herbert, dir. 1954. *Salt of the Earth*. Independent Productions.

Biggers, Jeff. 2006. *The United States of Appalachia*. Berkeley, Calif.: Counterpoint.

Billings, Dwight. 2016. "Hillbilly Elegy." *Occasional Links and Commentary on Economics, Culture and Society*. August 10, 2016. anticap.wordpress.com/2016/08/10/hillbilly-elegy/.

Billings, Dwight B., Gurney Norman, and Katherine Ledford, eds. 1999. *Confronting Appalachian Stereotypes: Back Talk from an American Region*. Lexington: University of Kentucky Press.

Bird, S. Elizabeth, ed. 1996. *Dressing in Feathers: The Construction of the Indian in American Popular Culture*. Boulder, Colo.: Westview.

Blauch, D. S. 1975. "Toward a Natural Delineation of the Area Known as the Southern Appalachian Highlands." *Castanea* 40, no. 3 (September): 197–201.

A Blue Ridge Romance. 1912. Los Angeles: Republic Pictures.

Bogle, Donald. 2001. *Toms, Coons, Mulattoes, Mammies, and Bucks: An Interpretive History of Blacks in American Films*. New expanded ed. New York: Continuum.

Boorman, John, dir. 1972. *Deliverance*. Burbank, Calif.: Warner Bros.

Borman, Kathryn M., and Phillip J. Obermiller. 1994. *From Mountain to Metropolis: Appalachian Migrants in American Cities*. Westport, Conn.: Bergen and Garvey.

Boyle, Deirdre. 1985. "Subject to Change: Guerrilla Television Revisited." *Art Journal* 45 (3): 228–32.

Bradner, Alexandra. 2013. "Buckwild or Hollow? Representing West Virginia through the Incommensurable Lenses of Justice and Care." *Journal of Appalachian Studies* 19, nos. 1–2 (Spring–Fall): 222–42.

Brosi, George. 2006. "Images and Icons." In *Encyclopedia of Appalachia*, edited by Rudy Abramson and Jean Haskell, 198–237. Knoxville: University of Tennessee Press.

Bryant, Felice, and Boudreaux Bryant. 1967. "Rocky Top." London: Decca/MCA, 1967.

Buscombe, Edward. 2006. *"Injuns!" Native Americans in the Movies*. London: Reaktion.

Butler, Michael D. 1976. "Narrative Structure and Historical Process in *The Last of the Mohicans*." *American Literature* 48 (2): 117–39.

Butts, Leonard C. 1979. "Nature in the Selected Works of Four Contemporary American Novelists." PhD diss., University of Tennessee.

Byrd, William, II. 1728. *The History of the Dividing Line betwixt Virginia and North Carolina*. Raleigh: North Carolina Historical Commission.

Cameron, Ardis. 2002. "When Strangers Bring Cameras: The Poetics and Politics of Othered Places." *American Quarterly* 54 (3): 411–35.

Campbell, John Charles. 1921. *The Southern Highlander and His Homeland*. New York: Sage.

Canby, Vincent. 1979. "Film: 'Norma Rae,' Mill-Town Story: Unionism in the South." *New York Times*, March 2, 1979.

Carroll, Shannon. 2013. "Hollow: An Interactive Documentary Made While in School, but It's No Student Film." PBS. September 6, 2013. www.pbs.org/pov/blog/tag/hollow/.

Caudill, Harry. 2001. *Night Comes to the Cumberlands: A Biography of a Depressed Area*. Ashland, Ky.: Stuart Foundation.

Churchill, Ward. 1992. *Fantasies of the Master Race: Literature, Cinema and the Colonization of American Indians*. Monroe, Maine: Common Courage.

Clabough, Casey Howard. 2002. *Elements: The Novels of James Dickey*. Macon, Ga.: Mercer University Press.

Cohen, David William. 2001. "The Fate of Documentation: The Ethics of Property in the Work of Visual Representation." *Kronos* 27:292–303.

Cooper, James Fenimore. 2003. *The Last of the Mohicans*. Philadelphia: Dover.

Corliss, Richard. 2012. "Lawless: A Crime Drama That's Remorseless—and Often Lifeless." *Time*, May 19, 2012.

Costa, Amanda Lin. 2013. "*Hollow*: The Next Step for Social Documentary?" *MediaShift*. September 26, 2013. http://mediashift.org/2013/09/hollow-the-next-step-for-social-documentary/.

Cox, Karen L. 2011. *Dreaming of Dixie: How the South Was Created in American Popular Culture*. Chapel Hill: University of North Carolina Press.

Cripps, Thomas. 1977. *Slow Fade to Black: The Negro in American Film, 1900–1942*. New York: Oxford University Press.

———. 1993. *Making Movies Black: The Hollywood Message Movie from World War II to the Civil Rights Era*. New York: Oxford University Press.

Crosley-Corcoran, Gina. 2014. "Explaining White Privilege to a Broke White Person." *Huffington Post*, May 8, 2014. huffingtonpost.com/gina-crosleycorcoran/explaining-white-privilege-to-a-broke-white-person_b_5269255.

Cukor, George, and Victor Fleming, dirs. 1939. *Gone with the Wind*. Burbank, Calif.: Warner Bros.

D'Agostino, Peter, and David Tafler, eds. 1995. *Transmission: Toward a Post-television Culture*. Thousand Oaks, Calif.: Sage.

Deloria, Philip J. 1998. *Playing Indian*. New Haven, Conn.: Yale University Press.

Derrida, Jacques. 1971. "Interview with Guy Scarpetta." In *Positions*. Chicago: University of Chicago Press.

Dickey, Christopher. 1999. *Summer of Deliverance: A Memoir of Father and Son*. New York: Touchstone.

Dickey, James. 1970. *Deliverance*. New York: Bantam.

Durand, Jorge, Douglas S. Massey, and Emilio A. Parrado. 1999. "The New Era of Mexican Migration to the United States." *Journal of American History* 86:518–36.

Dwan, Allan, dir. 1912a. *Blackened Hills*. Chicago: American Film.

———, dir. 1912b. *Wooers of Mountain Kate*. Chicago: American Film.

Dyer, Joyce. 1998. *Bloodroot: Reflections on Place by Appalachian Women Writers*. Lexington: University of Kentucky Press.

Dyer, Richard. 1997. *White*. London: Routledge.

Dykeman, Wilma. 1962. *The Tall Woman*. Newport, Tenn.: Wakestone Books.

Eller, Ronald D. 2008. *Uneven Ground: Appalachia since 1945*. Lexington: University of Kentucky Press.

Endel, Peggy Goodman. 1994. "Dickey, Dante, and the Demonic: Reassessing *Deliverance*." In Kirschten 1994, 175–86.

Engel, Mary Ella. 2010. "The Appalachian 'Granny': Testing the Boundaries of Female Power in Late-19th-Century Appalachian Georgia." *Appalachian Journal* 37 (3–4): 210–25.

Engelhardt, Elizabeth S. D. 2005. *Beyond Hill and Hollow: Original Readings in Appalachian Women's Studies*. Athens: Ohio University Press.

Farr, Sidney Saylor. 1981. *Appalachian Women: An Annotated Bibliography*. Lexington: University of Kentucky Press.

Feather, Carl E. 1998. *Mountain People in a Flat Land: A Popular History of Appalachian Migration to Northeast Ohio, 1940–1965*. Athens: Ohio University Press.

Ferguson, Mark Lynn. 2013. "Film Finds Faith in Coal Country: Exclusive Clip." *Revivalist*, June 20, 2013. www.therevivalist.info/hollow-documentary/.

Ferrence, Matthew J. 2014. *All-American Redneck: Variations on an Icon, from James Fenimore Cooper to the Dixie Chicks*. Knoxville: University of Tennessee Press.

Ford, Thomas R. 1962. *The Southern Appalachian Region: A Survey*. Lexington: University Press of Kentucky.

Frazier, Charles. 1997. *Cold Mountain*. New York: Grove.

Friar, Ralph E., and Natasha A. Friar. 1972. *The Only Good Indian*. New York: Drama Book Specialists.

Frost, William Goodell. 1899. "Our Contemporary Ancestors in the Southern Mountains." *Atlantic Monthly*, March 83, 1899, 311.

Gibson, Campbell J., and Emily Lennon. 2012. "Historical Census Statistics on the Foreign-Born Population of the United States: 1850–1990." Population Division, U.S. Census Bureau. Accessed November 10, 2017. www.census.gov/population/www/documentation/twps0029/twps0029.html.

Glen, John. 1989. "The War on Poverty in Appalachia: A Preliminary Report." *Register of the Kentucky Historical Society* 87 (1): 40–57.

Goings, Kenneth W. 1994. *Mammy and Uncle Mose: Black Collectibles and American Stereotyping*. Bloomington: Indiana University Press.

Granik, Debra, dir. 2010. *Winter's Bone*. Winter's Bone Production.

Green, Patricia. 1994. *Christy*. Los Angeles: MTM Entertainment.

Guerrero, Ed. 1993. *Framing Blackness: The African American Image in Film*. New York: Routledge.

Guy, Roger. 2007. *From Diversity to Unity: Southern and Appalachian Migrants in Uptown Chicago, 1950–1970*. Plymouth, U.K.: Lexington Books.

Hadley-Garcia, George. 1993. *Hispanic Hollywood: The Latins in Motion Pictures*. New York: Carol.

Hadley Torres, Nola. 2005. "Bringing My People Along: Urban Appalachian Women as Community Builders." In Engelhardt 2005, 50–74.

Haggis, Paul, dir. 2004. *Crash*. Los Angeles: Yari.

Hameed, Fatimah. 2013. "Mexican-American Miners Strike for Wage Justice in New Mexico, 1950–1952." Global Nonviolent Action Database, Swarthmore College. May 18, 2013. https://nvdatabase.swarthmore.edu/content/mexican-american-miners-strike-wage-justice-new-mexico-1950-1952.

Hanna, Stephen P. 1998. "Three Decades of Appalshop Films: Representational Strategies and Regional Politics." *Appalachian Journal* 25 (4): 372–413.

Harkins, Anthony. 2004. *Hillbilly: A Cultural History of an American Icon*. Oxford: Oxford University Press.

Hartigan, John, Jr. 2004. "Whiteness and Appalachian Studies: What's the Connection?" *Journal of Appalachian Studies* 10 (1–2): 58–72.

Hatton, Sara Day. 2005. *Teaching by Heart: The Foxfire Interviews*. New York: Teachers College Press.

Heilbrun, Carolyn. 1994. "The Masculine Wilderness of the American Novel." In Kirschten 1994, 59–60.

Herdman, Catherine N. 2013. "Appalshop Genesis: Appalachians Speaking for Themselves in the 1970s and 80s." PhD diss., University of Kentucky. Accessed November 20, 2017. http://uknowledge.uky.edu/history_etds/19.

Herndl, Diane Price. 2001. "Style and Sentimental Gaze in *Last of the Mohicans*." *Narrative* 9, no. 3 (October): 259–82.

Herzberg, Bob. 2008. *Savages and Saints: The Changing Image of American Indians in Westerns*. Jefferson, N.C.: McFarland.

Hilger, Michael. 1986. *The American Indian in Film*. Metuchen, N.J.: Scarecrow.

———. 1995. *From Savage to Nobleman: Images of Native Americans in Film*. Lanham, Md.: Scarecrow.

Hobbs, Stuart. 1998. Foreword to *Mountain People in a Flat Land: A Popular History of Appalachian Migration to Northeast Ohio, 1940–1965*. By Carl E. Feather. Athens: Ohio University Press.

Holden, Stephen. 2001. "A Tender Lady Explores Mountains and Their Music." *New York Times*, June 15, 2001.

Holt, J. B. 1940. "Holiness Religion: Cultural Shock and Social Reorganization." *American Sociological Review* 5:740–47.

hooks, bell. 1992. *Black Looks: Race and Representation*. Boston: South End.

———. 1996. *Reel to Real: Race, Sex and Class at the Movies*. London: Routledge.

House, Silas. 2015. "Deliver Me from 'Deliverance': Finally a Hollywood Movie Gets Appalachian People Right." *Salon*, October 25, 2015.

Howard, David, dir. 1932. *The Golden West*. Hollywood: Fox Film.

IDFA DocLab. 2013. "This Multimedia Collage Is a Morale Booster for the Residents of McDowell County, Who Keep Hope Alive in Their Shrinking Region." Accessed March 14, 2015. www.doclab.org/2013/hollow/.

Inge, M. Thomas. 2001. "Al Capp's South: Appalachian Humor in Lil Abner." *Studies in American Humor* 3 (8): 4–20.

Inscoe, John. 2005. *Appalachians and Race: The Mountain South from Slavery to Segregation*. Lexington: University of Kentucky Press.

Irvin, John, dir. 1989. *Next of Kin*. Los Angeles: Lorimar.

Jameson, Frederic. 1994. "The Great American Hunter, or Ideological Content in the Novel." In Kirschten 1994, 52–60.

Jay, Gregory S. 2000. "'White Man's Book No Good': D. W. Griffith and the American Indian." *Cinema Journal* 39 (4): 3–26.

Jefferson, Thomas. 1787. *Notes on the State of Virginia*. Avalon Project. Accessed November 17, 2017. http://avalon.law.yale.edu/18th_century/jeffvir.asp.

Johnson, Mark Steven, dir. 2013. *Killing Season*. Los Angeles: Millennium Films.

Johnson, Susan Allyn. 2000. "How the 'Rubber City' became the 'Capital of West Virginia': A Case Study of Early Appalachian Migration." *Journal of Appalachian Studies* 6 (1–2): 109–20.

Jones, J. R. 2013. "The Lost Chicago of *Medium Cool*." *Chicago Reader*, July 10, 2013.

Jones, Sarah. 2016. "J. D. Vance, the False Prophet of Blue America." *New Republic*, November 17, 2016.

Joyner, Nancy Carol. 1999. Review of *Bloodroot*. *NWSA Journal* 11 (3): 195–97.

Kahn, Kathy. 1972. *Hillbilly Women*. New York: Avon.

Kilpatrick, Jacquelyn. 1999. *Celluloid Indians: Native Americans and Film*. Lincoln: University of Nebraska Press.

Kirschten, Robert, ed. 1994. *Critical Essays on James Dickey*. New York: Hall.

Kotcheff, Ted, dir. 1989. *Winter People*. Los Angeles: Castle Rock.

Kranitz, Stacy. 2015. Artist statement. Excerpted in "Photos of Struggle and Hope in Appalachia." December 7, 2015. www.vice.com/en_us/article/ppx9vm/aint-no-grave-gonna-hold-my-body-down-v22n12.

Lacan, Jacques. 1997. *The Seminar Book III: The Psychoses, 1955–1956*. Translated by Russel Grigg. New York: Norton.

———. 2010. "The Mirror Stage." In *Social Theory: The Multicultural Readings*, edited by C. Lemert, 343–44. Philadelphia: Westview.

Latimer, Melissa, and Ann M. Oberhauser. 2004. "Exploring Gender and Economic Development in Appalachia." *Journal of Appalachian Studies* 10 (3): 269–91.

Lawrence, D. H. 1923. *Studies in Classic American Literature*. New York: Viking.

Lewis, Herschell Gordon, dir. 1964. *Two Thousand Maniacs*. Friedman-Lewis Productions.

Lindborg, Henry J. 1974. "James Dickey's *Deliverance*: The Ritual of Art." *Southern Literary Journal* 6 (2): 83–90.

Linkins, Jason. 2013. "West Virginia-Based Documentary Site 'Hollow' Has Launched, and It Is Magnificent." *Huffington Post*, June 20.

Lipsitz, George. 1995. "The Possessive Investment in Whiteness: Racialized Social Democracy and the White Problem in American Studies." *American Quarterly* 47 (September): 369–87.

Lundy, Ronni. 2014. "Appalachian Slumming." *Oxford American*. January 22, 2014. oxfordamerican.com.

MacGillis, Alec. 2016. "The Original Underclass." *Atlantic*, September 2016.

Madge of the Mountains. 1911. Brooklyn, N.Y.: Vitagraph Studios.

Maggard, Sally Ward. 1999. "Coalfield Women Making History." In Billings, Norman, and Ledford 1999, 228–50.

Mann, Michael, dir. 1992. *The Last of the Mohicans*. Santa Monica, Calif: Morgan Creek Entertainment.

Marin, Cheech, dir. 1987. *Born in East L.A.* N.p.: Clear Type.

Marin, Daniel B. 1970. "James Dickey's *Deliverance*: Darkness Visible." Reprinted in *James Dickey: The Expansive Imagination*, edited by Richard J. Calhoun, 105–17. Deland, Fla.: Everett/Edwards, 1973.

Martin, Terence. 1969. "From the Ruins of History: 'The Last of the Mohicans.'" *Novel: A Forum on Fiction* 2 (3): 221–29.

Maslin, Janet. 1994. "Nell: A Woman within a Wild Child, as Revealed by Jodie Foster." *New York Times*, December 14, 1994.

Mason, Carol. 2009. *Reading Appalachia Left to Right*. Ithaca: Cornell University Press.

McCarroll, Meredith. 2014. "Consuming Performances: Race, Media, and the Failure of the Cultural Mulatto in *Bamboozled* and *Erasure*." In *Passing Interest: Racial Passing in US Novels, Memoirs, Television, and Film, 1990–2010*, edited by Julie Cary Nerad, 283–306. Albany: State University New York Press.

McClintock, Anne. 1995. *Imperial Leather: Race, Gender and Sexuality in the Colonial Contest*. London: Routledge.

McElya, Micki. 2007. *Clinging to Mammy: The Faithful Slave in Twentieth-Century America*. Cambridge, Mass.: Harvard University Press.

McGowan, Todd. 2003. "Looking for the Gaze: Lacanian Film Theory and Its Vicissitudes." *Cinema Journal* 42 (3): 27–47.

McIntosh, Peggy. 2001. "White Privilege: Unpacking the Invisible Knapsack." In *White Privilege: Essential Readings on the Other Side of Racism*, edited by Paula S. Rothenberg, 97–101. New York: Worth.

McMillion Sheldon, Elaine. 2013a. *Hollow: An Interactive Documentary*. Hollow Interactive. Accessed November 20, 2017. www.hollowdocumentary.com.

———. 2013b. "The New Digital Storytelling Series: Elaine McMillion." *Filmmaker*, March 14, 2013. http://filmmakermagazine.com/66938-the-new-digital -storytelling-series-elaine-mcmillion/#.VQRjuq1dVkg.

———. 2013c. "West Virginia, Still Home." *New York Times*, June 20, 2013.

———. 2014. "The Power of Collaboration and Using Technology Wisely." DC Web and Digital Media Festival. October 14, 2014. www.youtube.com/watch?v= c4LoPEEfAgQ.

Méliès, Gaston. 1910. *A Mountain Wife*. San Antonio: Star Film.

Mendible, Myra, ed. 2007. *From Bananas to Buttocks: The Latina Body in Popular Film and Culture*. Austin: University of Texas Press.

Miller, Danny L. 1996. *Wingless Flights: Appalachian Women in Fiction*. Bowling Green, Ohio: Bowling Green State University Popular Press.

Minghella, Anthony, dir. 2003. *Cold Mountain*. Santa Monica, Calif.: Miramax.

Morrison, Toni. 1992. *Playing in the Dark: Whiteness and the Literary Imagination*. New York: Vintage.

———. 1994. *The Bluest Eye*. New York: Plume.

Moynihan, Daniel Patrick. 1965. *The Negro Family: The Case for National Action*. Washington, D.C.: U.S. Department of Labor, Office of Policy Planning and Research.

Mulvey, Laura. 1975. "Visual Pleasure and Narrative Cinema." In Thornham 1999, 58–69.

Nelson, Gary, dir. 1981. *The Pride of Jesse Hallam*. Hollywood: Konigsberg.

Norris, Randall, and Jean-Philippe Cyprès. 1996. *Women of Coal*. Lexington: University of Kentucky Press.

Obermiller, Phillip J. 2011. "Migration." In *High Mountains Rising: Appalachia in Time and Place*, edited by Richard A. Straw and H. Tyler Blethen, 88–100. Urbana: University of Illinois Press.

Obermiller, Phillip J., and Michael Maloney. 2016. "The Uses and Misuses of Appalachian Culture." *Journal of Appalachian Studies* 22 (1): 103–12.

Obermiller, Phillip J., and William Philliber. 2017. *Too Few Tomorrows: Urban Appalachians in the 1980s*. Chapel Hill: Appalachian State University/University of North Carolina Press.

O'Connor, John E. 1980. *The Hollywood Indian*. Paterson, N.J.: New Jersey State Museum.

Omi, Michael, and Howard Whisnant. 2014. *Racial Formation in the United States*. London: Routledge.

Ono, Kenty, and Vincent Pham. 2009. *Asian Americans and the Media*. Cambridge, Mass.: Polity.

Patterson, Marvin Breckinridge, dir. 1931. *The Forgotten Frontier*. Washington, D.C.: Durrin.

Petrie, Daniel, dir. 1994. *The Dollmaker*. Los Angeles: Finnegan Productions.

Petty, Miriam. 2016. *Stealing the Show: African American Performers and Audiences in 1930s Hollywood*. Oakland: University of California Press.

Philliber, William W., and Clyde B. McCoy. 1981. *The Invisible Minority: Urban Appalachians*. Lexington: University Press of Kentucky.

Pilgrim, David. 2012. "The Mammy Caricature." Accessed November 9, 2017. https://ferris.edu/HTMLS/news/jimcrow/mammies/homepage.htm.

Pollard, Kelvin M. 2005. *Population Growth and Distribution in Appalachia: New Realities*. Washington, D.C.: Appalachian Regional Commission.

Powell, Douglas Reichert. 2007. *Critical Regionalism: Connecting Politics and Culture in the American Landscape*. Chapel Hill: University of North Carolina Press.

Price, Diane, Ruth Ellen Blakeney, Donavan Cain, et al. 2000. "A Camera Is a Gun: A Discussion of *Stranger with a Camera*" *Appalachian Journal* 27 (4): 406–17.

Raine, James Watt. 1924. *The Land of Saddle-Bags: A Study of the Mountain People of Appalachia*. N.p.: Council of Women for Home Missions and Missionary Education Movement of the United States and Canada.

Ralph, Julian. 1903. "Our Appalachian Americans." *Harper's New Monthly Magazine* 107 (637): 32–41.

Ramírez Berg, Charles. 2002. *Latino Images in Film: Stereotypes, Subversion, and Resistance*. Austin: University of Texas Press.

Rasmussen, Birgit Brander, Irene J. Nexica, Matt Wray, and Eric Klinenberg, eds. 2001. *The Making and Unmaking of Whiteness*. Durham, N.C.: Duke University Press.

Reed, John Shelton. 1986. *Southern Folk, Plain and Fancy: Native White Social Types*. Athens: University of Georgia Press.

Rhines, Jesse Algernon. 1996. *Black Film/White Money*. New Brunswick, N.J.: Rutgers University Press.

Rice, Connie Park, and Marie Tedesco. 2016. *Women of the Mountain South: Identity, Work, and Activism*. Athens: Ohio University Press.

Robbins, Jerome, and Robert Wise, dirs. 1961. *West Side Story*. New York: Mirisch.

Rodriquez, Clara. 2004. *Heroes, Lovers, and Others: The Story of Latinos in Hollywood*. Oxford: Oxford University Press.

Rollins, Peter. 2011. *Hollywood's Indian: The Portrayal of the Native American in Film*. Lexington: University Press of Kentucky.

Romalis, Shelly. 1999. *Pistol Packin' Mama: Aunt Molly Jackson and the Politics of Folksong*. Champaign-Urbana: University of Illinois Press.

Rosenblum, Marc R., William A. Kandel, Clare Ribando Seelke, and Ruth Ellen Wasem. 2012. "Mexican Migration to the United States: Policy and Trends." Congressional Research Service 7-5700. June 7, 2012. www.crs.gov.

Ryan, William. 1976. *Blaming the Victim*. New York: Vintage.

Rydell, Mark, dir. 1984. *The River*. Universal City, Calif: Universal Pictures.

Said, Edward. 1978. *Orientalism*. New York: Pantheon.

Schmidt, Rob, dir. 2003. *Wrong Turn*. Santa Monica, Calif: Summit Entertainment.

Schwarzweller, Harry, James Brown, and J. J. Mangalam. 1971. *Mountain Families in Transition: A Case Study of Appalachian Migration*. Philadelphia: Pennsylvania State University Press.

Scorsese, Martin, dir. 1991. *Cape Fear*. Universal City, Calif: Amblin Entertainment.

Scott, A. O. 2012. "Moonshine County That Is Stirred, Not Shaken." *New York Times*, August 28, 2012.

See America First. 1915. Buffalo, N.Y.: Pathe Exchange.

Sensational Logging. 1910. Chicago: Essanay Film.

Shaheen, Jack. 2009. *Reel Bad Arabs: How Hollywood Vilifies a People*. Northhampton, Mass.: Interlink Books.

Shamberg, Michael. 1971. *Guerilla Television*. New York: Holt.

Sheppard, Muriel Earley. 1991 *Cabins in the Laurel*. Chapel Hill: University of North Carolina Press.

Sherman, Mandel, and Thomas E. Henry. 1933. *Hollow Folk*. Berryville: Virginia Book Company.

Shields, Juliet. 2009. "Savage and Scott-ish Masculinity in *The Last of the Mohicans* and *The Prairie*: James Fenimore Cooper and the Diasporic Origins of American Identity." *Nineteenth-Century Literature* 64 (2): 137–62.

Slotkin, Richard. 1973. *Regeneration through Violence: The Mythology of the American Frontier, 1600–1860*. Norman: University of Oklahoma Press.

Smith, Barbara Ellen. 1999. "'Beyond the Mountains': The Paradox of Women's Place in Appalachian History." *NWSA Journal* 11, no. 3 (Fall): 1–17.

———. 2004. "De-gradations of Whiteness: Appalachia and the Complexities of Race." *Journal of Appalachian Studies* 10 (nos. 1–2): 38–57.

Smith, John. 1624. *The Generall Historie of Virginia, New-England, and the Summer Isles*. Accessed November 20, 2017. http://docsouth.unc.edu/southlit/smith/smith.html.

Smith, Rend. 2008. "Survival and Resistance: Appalshop's First 40 Years." *National Alliance for Media and Culture*. December 19, 2008. namac.org/mode/6630.

Sohn, Katherine Kelleher. 2006. *Whistlin' and Crowin' Women of Appalachia: Literacy Practices since College*. Carbondale: Southern Illinois University Press.

"Southern Folklife Collection." 2017. Louis Round Wilson Library Special Collections, University of North Carolina. Accessed November 20, 2017. www.unc.edu/%7Ewhisnant/appal/maps/Appreg.gif.

Spivak, Gayatri Chakravorty. 1988. "Can the Subaltern Speak?" In *Marxism and the Interpretation of Culture*, edited by Cary Nelson and Lawrence Grossberg, 271–313. London: Macmillan.

Steele, Ian. 1993. Review of *The Last of the Mohicans*. *Journal of American History* 80 (3): 1179–81.

Stephenson, Jane B. 1996. *Courageous Paths: Stories of Nine Appalachian Women*. Berea, Ky.: New Opportunity School for Women.

St. John, Maria. 1999. "'It Ain't Fittin': Cinematic and Fantasmatic Contours of Mammy in *Gone with the Wind* and Beyond." *Qui Parle* 11 (2): 127–36.

Stowe, Harriet Beecher. 1966. *Uncle Tom's Cabin*. New York: New American Library.

Thornham, Sue, ed. 1999. *Feminist Film Theory: A Reader*. Edinburgh, Scotland: Edinburgh University Press.

Travers, Peter. 2012. "Lawless Review." *Rolling Stone*, August 30.

Tucker, Bruce. 2003. "Harry Caudill and the Problem of the Past." *Journal of Appalachian Studies* 9 (1): 114–46.

Turan, Kenneth. 1994. "'Nell': From, but Not of, This World." *Los Angeles Times*, December 14.

Turner, William, and Edward J. Cabbell. 1985. *Blacks in Appalachia*. Lexington: University of Kentucky Press.

USDA. 1935. *Economic and Social Problems and Conditions of the Southern Appalachians*. Washington, D.C.: GPO.

Valdez, Avelardo, and Jeffrey A. Halley. 1999. "Teaching Mexican American Experiences through Film: Private Issues and Public Problems." *Teaching Sociology* 27 (3): 286–95.

Valdez, Luis, dir. 1981. *Zoot Suit*. Universal City, Calif: Universal Pictures.

Vance, J. D. 2016. *Hillbilly Elegy*. New York: Harper.

Van Ness, Gordon. 1993. "'The Whole Situation Was Mine': James Dickey's Fictional Protagonists and the Ethics of Survival." *James Dickey Newsletter* 10, no. 1 (Fall): 17.

Van Pelt, Tamise. 1997. "Lacan in Context: An Introduction to Lacan for the English-Speaking Reader." *College Literature* 24, no. 2 (June): 57–70.

Wallace-Sanders, Kimberly. 2008. *Mammy: A Century of Race, Gender, and Southern Memory*. Ann Arbor: University of Michigan Press.

Weiler, A. H. 1960. "Kazan Film Is Drawn from Two Novels." *New York Times*, May 27, 1960.

Weller, Jack. 1965. *Yesterday's People: Life in Contemporary Appalachia*. Lexington: University Press of Kentucky.

Wellman, William A., dir. 1952. *My Man and I*. Los Angeles: Metro-Goldwyn-Mayer.

Werth, James L., Jr. 2014. "How the War on Poverty Became the War on the Poor: Central Appalachia as a Case Example." *SES Indicator* 7 (1): www.apa.org/pi/ses/resources/indicator/2014/01/index.aspx.

Wexler, Haskell, dir. 1969. *Medium Cool*. Hollywood: Paramount Pictures.

———. 2013. *Medium Cool*. New York: Criterion Collection.

Whisnant, David E. 1983. *All That Is Native and Fine: The Politics of Culture in an American Region*. Chapel Hill: University of North Carolina Press.

———. n.d. *Appalachian Region Borders*. University of North Carolina at Chapel Hill. Accessed November 19, 2017. www.unc.edu/~whisnant/appal/maps/Appreg.gif.

White, Stephen E. 1989. "America's Soweto." *Appalachian Journal* 16, no 4 (Summer): 350–60.

Williams, John Alexander. 2001. "Appalachia History: Regional History in the Post-Modern Zone." *Appalachian Journal* 28, no 2 (Winter): 168–87.

———. 2002. *Appalachia: A History*. Chapel Hill: University of North Carolina Press.

Williams, Linda. 1980. "Type and Stereotype: Chicano Images in Film." *Frontiers: A Journal of Women Studies* 5, no. 2: 14–17.

Williamson, Jerry W. 1994. *Southern Mountaineers in Silent Films*. Jefferson, N.C.: McFarland.

———. 1995a. *Hillbillyland: What the Movies Did to the Mountains and What the Mountains Did to the Movies*. Chapel Hill: University of North Carolina Press.

———. 1995b. *Southern Mountaineers Filmography*. Special Collections at Belk Library. Accessed November 17, 2017. www.collections.library.appstate.edu/ southernmountaineersfilmography.

Wilson, Darlene. 1995. "The Felicitous Convergence of Mythmaking and Capital Accumulation." *Journal of Appalachian Studies* 1 (Fall): 5–44.

Winkler, Henry, dir. 1986. *Smoky Mountain Christmas*. 1986. New York: CBS/Fox.

"Winner 2013: Hollow Interactive, LCC." 2013. *Peabody: Stories That Matter*. Grady College of Journalism and Mass Communication, University of Georgia. Accessed November 19, 2017. www.peabodyawards.com/award-profile/hollow -www.hollowdocumentary.com.

"W. L. Eury Appalachian Collection." 2017. Appalachian State University. Accessed November 20, 2017. www.collections.library.appstate.edu/appalachian/maps.

Wray, Matt. 2006. *Not Quite White: White Trash and the Boundaries of Whiteness*. Durham, N.C.: Duke University Press.

York, Ashley, and Sally Rubin, dirs. Forthcoming. *Hillbilly: Appalachia in Film and Television*. Los Angeles: Holler Home.

Index

Printed in the USA
CPSIA information can be obtained
at www.ICGtesting.com
CBHW010004071224
18635CB00008B/225